# Walks

# Mysterious Cheshire

## Fifteen walks through Cheshire's historic countryside

by
**Tony Bowerman**

THISTLE
BOOKS

First Impression 1990, Reprinted 1991.
Copyright © 1989 Tony Bowerman.

Published by Thistle Books
Chiltern Cottage, Gayton Lane, Gayton,
Wirral, Merseyside, L60 3SH.

Book design and maps by Thistle Books.
Cover design by Kerry Maddrell.
Cover Photographs - White Nancy, Bollington (front);
Packhorse bridge, Hockenhull Platts and the tomb at
Plemstall Church, Little Barrow (back) - by P.K.Griffiths.
Other photographs by the Author unless otherwise credited.

Printed and bound in Great Britain by Eaton Press,
Wirral, Merseyside.

ISBN 0 9515739 0 X

A CIP catalogue record for this book is available from the British Library

**Conditions of Sale**

# Acknowledgements

The long process of writing a book involves the assistance of many people. In particular I should like to thank the staff of the Chester Reference Library and the Cheshire County Records Office, whose knowledge and freely-given help has been invaluable.

Others to whom thanks are due include: Sue Brown for the kind loan of her Peaks' cottage; Jean Ashley for graphics advice; Mr Platt of Eddisbury Hill Farm; the Shocklach church-wardens; the Gooseberry Lane residents, Willington; Manchester Museum for first-hand accounts of digging up the bog man; the Forestry Commission Polyhouse Unit at Delamere; Barrow Nurseries Ltd, Little Barrow; Barhill Development Farm, Tushingham; the owner of Laundry Cottage, Peckforton, for kind permission to photograph from her garden; the National Trust warden at Alderley Edge; and various friends for their encouragement and for testing the walks.

The two lines of a poem that appear in walk 7 Bickerton ~ *from Mad Allen's Hole to the Maiden's Castle,* are from Siegfried Sassoon's *'On Scratchbury Camp'.*

While neither the author nor publisher can accept responsibility for errors and omissions, great care has been taken to ensure the guide is factually correct. The author would appreciate constructive comments from readers. (Letters should be addressed to the publishers, Thistle Books, Chiltern Cottage, Gayton Lane, Gayton, Wirral, Merseyside L60 3SH.)

The maps in this book are based upon the Ordnance Survey 6in to 1 mile maps with the permission of the Controller of HMSO © Crown Copyright.

# Contents

# Introduction ~

## What is so mysterious about Cheshire?

In the balm of summer or on a bright, crisp day in winter I sit sometimes on one of Cheshire's higher hills - Beeston Crag, Helsby Hill or Congleton Cloud - and gaze out over the plain. From such a vantage point a single question always puzzles me: what did the landscape stretched out below look like in the distant past? How much was forest and woodland? How much was swamp and marsh? Where did the old roads and tracks run? Where were the first villages and towns? What did Cheshire look like to our ancestors?

All the clues are there, in our modern, increasingly ephemeral landscape. Clues that will tell us how things used to be. They are waiting only to be uncovered. And by walking in that landscape, with our eyes open, we can take a closer look. *'Walks in Mysterious Cheshire'* is just that: an attempt to trace Cheshire's past, to explore the last hidden corners, to get a sense of history, and to wring out the remnants of a vanishing way of life - old Cheshire, before the pace of progress removes them forever. Take that chance while you can, for the face of the countryside will alter soon beyond recognition.

Anyone who completes all the walks - and I hope there will be a few more than just me, who was obliged to walk each of them at least twice - should have a better understanding at the end of what has made Cheshire the county of diversity that it is today. Go forth and walk!

## What shall I see?

### Cheshire ~ north, south, east and west.

The fifteen walks are spread across the county from Shocklach on the

Welsh marches in the west, to Three Shires Head, Bollington and Congleton on the upland hills of the Peak District in the east. To the north, the walk from Little Barrow looks at the isolated church at Plemstall; and, in the south, another walk takes in the lost chapel in the fields at Tushingham. Other walks explore the sandstone spine of the county at Bickerton, Peckforton, Willington and Delamere. And there are walks alongside the rivers Dee, Gowy, Weaver, Dane and Dean. The choice is yours.

## Cheshire ~ county of mysteries.

Each walk features at least one mysterious, unexplained Cheshire peculiarity. Some walks contain several. Among them are a whole catalogue of the unusual:

> *A ghostly duck, a mummified rat, a stone elephant, 'Pete Marsh' - the bog man, a cavalier's hat, a lost Roman bronze diploma, the Nun's Grave, the grave of the 'King of the Gypsies', a hermit's cave, a ghostly procession, a Neolithic burial chamber, a Saxon holy well, a lost chapel, a church in the marshes, a vanished Medieval abbey, the oldest Primitive Methodist chapel, a Gospel Oak, Iron Age hillforts, a Dark Ages stronghold, Roman roads, a Norman castle, a plague stone, the Black Lake, an ancient peat moss, a hanging path, saltways, sunken ways, green lanes, packhorse routes, packhorse bridges, a bottomless pit, copper mines, stone quarries, marl pits, tunnels and caves, 'White Nancy', witchcraft, a thieves' rendezvous, the home of Nixon the Cheshire prophet, the Wizard's Well from the legend of the Wizard of Alderley Edge ... and much more.*

## Cheshire ~ reminders of the past

*'**Walks in Mysterious Cheshire**'* covers the vast span of the county's past. From the Ice Ages through the Neolithic, Bronze Age,

Iron Age, and Roman period to the Dark Ages, Norman Conquest, Middle Ages, Tudor period and Civil War and on to the Industrial Revolution and the present day. And for each period, there is something to see or touch or explore. Something to make you wonder. Something mysterious.

# Walking in the Countryside

### Finding your way

Each walk is clearly described. To make route-finding as a easy as possible, a fourfold system of directions has been used:

* **A simple map** shows the route for each walk. It also shows the main features of the route, and anything of particular interest.

* **An information box** at the start of each walk shows where it begins, its length, a guide to the time necessary, which Ordnance Survey (OS) maps (either the Landranger 1:50,000 [2 cms to the kilometre]; or the 1:25,000 [4 cms to the kilometre] maps) you should take with you, and the kind of country you'll be crossing. It also lists a pub where food and drink can be found.

* **The main text** describes not only the countryside and what to look out for, but also gives full directions of the route. Left and right are abbreviated to L and R, to help you keep track.

* **Map references** provide a fourth safeguard to ensure you are on the right path. They are given for the start of the walk, alongside the text for each major turning or feature, and for the pub or restaurant at the end of the walk.

## Reading an OS Map

Because each of the walks is short (between 1.5 and 4.5 miles, 2.5 to 7 kilometres), you can do the routes in *'Walks in Mysterious Cheshire'* just by following the directions in this book. Even so, there are good reasons to take a map with you. Understanding a map and map-reading will greatly add to your enjoyment, show you where you are and where you are going, and open up a new appreciation of the countryside. Ordnance Survey maps are precision instruments and show a great deal - from footpaths, forests and rivers to battlefields, Ancient Monuments and interesting place-names. They can also identify landmarks or make sense of a distant view. Without a map you will be missing many of the interesting clues hidden in the landscape.

Most of the fifteen walks appear on just two Ordnance Survey maps in the 1:50,000 Landranger Series - Sheet 117 Chester, and Sheet 118 Stoke-on-Trent and Macclesfield area. The scale of 1:50,000 is 2 cms to the kilometre, or just over 1 inch to the mile. This scale is sufficient for route-finding in most areas.

Larger scale, 1:25,000 maps provide more detail and include field boundaries. The numbers of these maps appear in the information box, after the number of the main 1:50,000 map, as, for example: SJ 45. Both kinds of maps are available through bookshops. They can also be borrowed or consulted at the larger libraries.

Understanding or reading a map is quite simple. Study the map at home until you become familiar with the main symbols: contours, roads, footpaths, bridleways, streams, and so on. Once in the field, 'set' your map so that it is orientated in the direction you are heading. The top of the map points north; so if you are heading south, you should have it upside down. Try to keep track of where you are on the map as you go along. If in doubt, identify two or three features on the ground, and then find them on the map - this should confirm your position.

The map references in the text refer to specific points on the map. If you are in doubt as to where you should be according to the text, then check your position on the map against the map reference which is given alongside each main paragraph.

## Following an OS Map Reference

This is easier than it sounds. The idea of a grid reference is the same as that used in the well-known game of 'Battleships'; but in this case, instead of identifying a square by the coordinates A4 or C10 for example, the Ordnance Survey uses a slightly more complex, but more exact system with two sets of three figures - the first three for the across reference, and the last three for the up reference. They are usually shown as a continuous six figure number.

On the Chester map, for example, the OS map reference for Chester Cathedral is **SJ 406665.**

The initial letters SJ refer to a particular 100,000 metre square area of the National Grid. This identifies the part of the Country and ties in with particular maps.

Next, you will see the map is divided into 1 km squares by a grid of pale blue lines. Each of these lines is numbered, both horizontally and vertically. A map reference, as given in the text, is made up of two sets of three figures, listed one after the other. Of this six-figure number, the first three figures refer to the *Eastings*, or across reference. While the last three figures refer to the *Northings* or up reference. Put together they give a grid reference.

To find a specific location, first take the initial three figures. These are the *Eastings* or across reference. The first two correspond to the large blue figures that run along the top and bottom of the map (they also appear across the map at 10 kilometre intervals). The third figure refers to the number of tenths across the square to the right of this vertical grid line. This tells you that the point you are trying to find is somewhere on this vertical line.

Follow the same procedure for the up reference or *Northing* using the second set of three figures given in the grid reference. This time the reference numbers run up the map on either side, and also up the middle (again at 10 kilometre intervals). This will give you a horizontal line along which the point you are looking for is to be found.

Work out where the two lines cross and you should have the point you are looking for.

If all this sounds rather complex, try it out using a map. If it still seems difficult, look at the OS explanation which appears in a box beneath the list of symbols attached to each map. You'll soon get the hang of it; and it's a skill worth learning.


## Rights of Way

Public footpaths are a very British feature; with over 120,000 miles (192,000 kilometres) of footpaths in England and Wales, we have more than any other country. In Scotland, walkers enjoy even greater freedom of access. While, in places like Sweden and Switzerland the public have the right to wander where they please in the countryside, subject only to local laws and the understanding that no damage is done.

So the English or Welsh footpath is both a freedom and a restriction. In Britain all land is owned by someone - an individual or a corporate body, and the walker has often to keep to specific routes and rights of way.

A right of way is just that: a right to cross someone's land. The landowner may properly object if the walker does damage or leaves litter. If a walker strays from the right of way he is trespassing, and can be sued for damages.

~~~~~~~~~~~~~~~~~~~~~~~~~~~~~~~~~~~~~~~~~~~~~~~~~~~~~~~~

There are several categories of path:

* Public footpaths, for use on foot only - sometimes waymarked in yellow.

* Bridleways, for use on foot, horseback or pedal cycle - sometimes waymarked in blue.

* Byways (usually old roads), most 'Roads Used As Public Paths', and public roads, for use by all traffic including motor vehicles.

Most paths for which there is right of way should be shown on Ordnance Survey maps. Footpaths are shown on OS maps as red-dotted lines (or in green on the 1:25,000 Outdoor Leisure maps). In addition, paths and tracks that are not designated for public use are indicated in black; there may be access agreements or 'permissive' use on such paths. You may also use by local or established custom or consent some: areas of open moorland, commons, canal towpaths, Country Parks, private paths and tracks, and woods and forests, especially those belonging to the Forestry Commission.

County councils, including Cheshire County Council, keep 'definitive maps', which show all the public footpaths, bridleways and tracks. They can be consulted in public libraries, (in the reference library at Chester, for example). All the walks in this book are based upon routes shown on these definitive maps.

On rights of way you can:

* Take a shorter route round an illegal obstructon, or remove it sufficiently to get past.

* Take a dog on a lead or under close control.

* Take a pushchair, pram, invalid carriage or wheelchair if practicable.

Fuller advice is given in a free 40 page booklet, 'Out in the Country', available from: The Countryside Commission Publications Despatch Department, 19-23 Albert Road, Manchester, M19 2EQ.


## The Country Code

This is the updated, 12 point, 1982 version of the code:

- \* Enjoy the countryside and respect its life and work.
- \* Guard against all risk of fire.
- \* Fasten all gates.
- \* Keep dogs under close control.
- \* Keep to public footpaths across farmland.
- \* Use gates and stiles to cross fences, hedges and walls.
- \* Leave livestock, crops and machinery alone.
- \* Take your litter home.
- \* Help keep all water clean.
- \* Protect wildlife, plants and trees.
- \* Take special care on country roads.
- \* Make no unnecessary noise.


## What to Wear and What to Take

All the routes in *'Walks in Mysterious Cheshire'* are short and essentially easy. Nonetheless, proper footwear and clothing, along with a few other tips, will make walking that much easier and more pleasant.

During the summer many of these walks can be completed happily in trainers or ordinary shoes; while in the winter wellington boots may be a good idea. But you can't beat proper walking boots for comfort and reliability. Walking boots have a breathable but fairly waterproof leather upper and a well constructed sole that gives better grip than most other kinds of shoe. They also support and protect the ankles, preventing sprains.

As far as clothes are concerned, the important factors are comfort and warmth. It's best to be prepared for the worst likely conditions: carry an extra pullover, waterproofs, a hat and gloves with you in a rucksack. A number of layers that can be added to or shed, depending on conditions, are better than a few heavier clothes. Experienced walkers adopt a three or four layer system: thermal underwear (in winter), shirt, pullover or zip-fronted pile-fibre jacket and a top 'shell' layer or waterproof and windproof over-jacket with integral hood. Similarly, on the bottom half wear thermal long-johns (in winter), loose, comfortable trousers (avoid jeans), thermal and carry a pair of waterproof overtrousers.

Zip-up gaiters that protect the top of your boots and the bottom of your trousers are surprisingly useful; I recommend them.

Other things to take in the rucksack include: maps, a litre of water or a thermos in winter, some food, a compass, binoculars or a camera, and perhaps a notebook. A waterproof map case (which is very cheap) is also worth having; they stop maps getting soggy, or damaged by constantly being stuffed into pockets.

# Key to the maps in this book

| | | | |
|---|---|---|---|
| 🍄 🍄 | deciduous trees | **P.H.** | public house |
| ↟ ↟ | pines | ⤬ | bridge |
| ☀ | tumulus, tump | △ | triangulation point |
| ⌇ | precipice, cliff | ▦ | castle |
| ~ | stream, river | Ⱳ Ⱳ | bog, marsh |
| ✝ | church, chapel | **P** | parking |
| ▨ | building | ⫢ | station |
| (ᴡᴡ) | lake, pool | ⫽ | slope, hillside |
| ↗ | path, route | ⁕ | overhead powerlines |
| ↙ | (return route) | ⫽ | road, lane |
| ✚✚✚ | railway | ······ | track |

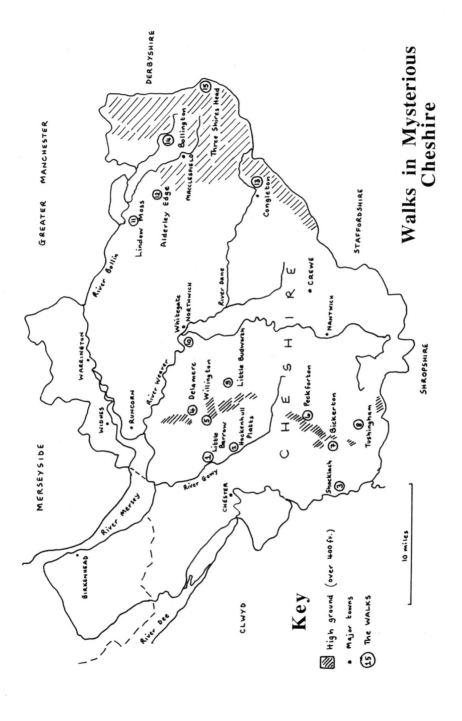

# Walks in Mysterious Cheshire

GREATER MANCHESTER

DERBYSHIRE

MERSEYSIDE

STAFFORDSHIRE

SHROPSHIRE

CLWYD

CHESHIRE

River Mersey

River Dee

River Gowy

River Weaver

River Bollin

River Dane

BIRKENHEAD

WIDNES

WARRINGTON

RUNCORN

CHESTER

CREWE

NANTWICH

NORTHWICH

MACCLESFIELD

Lindow Moss

Alderley Edge

Bollington

Three Shires Head

Congleton

Whitegate

Delamere

Willington

Little Budworth

Little Barrow

Hockenhull Platts

Peckforton

Bickerton

Tushingham

Shocklach

① Little Barrow
② Hockenhull Platts
③ Shocklach
④ Delamere
⑤ 
⑥ Peckforton
⑦ Bickerton
⑧ Tushingham
⑨ Little Budworth
⑩ 
⑪ Lindow Moss
⑫ Alderley Edge
⑬ Congleton
⑭ Bollington
⑮ Three Shires Head

## Key

High ground (over 400 ft.)

• Major towns

⑮ The WALKS

10 miles

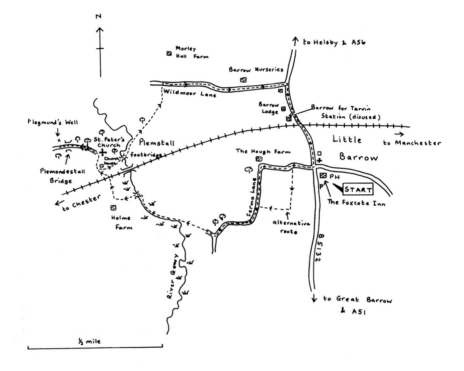

N

to Helsby & A56

Morley
Hall Farm

Barrow Nurseries

Wildmoor Lane

Barrow
Lodge

Barrow for Tarvin
Station (disused)

Plegmund's Well

St. Peter's
Church

Plemstall

footbridge

Little

Barrow

to Manchester

The Hough Farm

Plemondestall
Bridge

Church
House

to Chester

Holme
Farm

Ferma Lane

alternative
route

PH

START

P

The Foxcote Inn

B5132

to Great Barrow
& A51

River Gowy

½ mile

**Little Barrow**

# 1 Little Barrow ~ *across the Gowy Marshes* ~

**Hilltop settlement, sunken green lanes, across the flatlands, the River Gowy, isolated Plemstall Church, footbridges and local memories.**

**Start:** *Little Barrow 4 miles (6.5 kilometres) east of Chester. Map reference* **SJ 470699.**
**Distance**: *3 miles (5 kilometres).*
**Duration:** *3 hours.*
**Maps**: *OS 1:50,000 Landranger Sheet 117 Chester;*
*OS 1:25,000 SJ 46 & 47.*
**Terrain**: *Mostly flat; one descent and one ascent. Green lanes, farm tracks, field paths; muddy at times.*
**Food and Drink**: *The Foxcote Inn Station Lane, Little Barrow. Map reference* **SJ 470699.** *Greenall Whitley. Bar snacks and hot food. Open all day in summer. Tel: Mickle Trafford 301145.*

Travellers by boat up the Mersey in pre-Roman times would have seen a deeply cut bay on the southern shore where Cheshire's River Gowy pushed its waters out into the tide. Most of them paddled on to enter the Weaver, for landing before that on the Cheshire bank was virtually impossible. The slow-flowing Gowy falls only 280 feet (90 metres) from its source beneath the Peckforton Hills; and much of its lower course was a broad, waterlogged marshland, extending inland to what is now Huxley, and beyond.

A maze of streams, swamp and peat moss, the Gowy marshes effectively cut northern Cheshire in half. Wind-combed reed-beds full of ducks, geese, bitterns and herons were fringed by water-loving alders and willows; eels and otters coexisted in the gutters, and harriers quartered the marshes on the lookout for unwary prey. It was a wilderness teeming with life; a wilderness ripe with possibility for Man.

Settlements grew up on each scrap of high ground. The name Ince - an ancient village near the Gowy's mouth - comes from the Welsh *ynys* meaning island. Elton, Thornton and Stoak were other early settlements. While Plemstall - *Plegmund's Stow*, the hermitage of Plegmund - was another island which probably hosted an Anglo-Saxon wooden church during the Dark Ages. Equally remote was the Norman abbey at Stanlow, near the Gowy's mouth; but in 1279 and again in 1287 it was flooded out, the buildings submerged and access by land cut off. In response to piteous appeals, the Pope moved the monks to Lancashire. Living amidst the Gowy Marshes was never easy.

**SJ 470699**   Our walk begins at the hilltop village of Little Barrow, 4 miles (7 kms) north-east of Chester, overlooking the broad flood-plain of the Gowy. The name Barrow comes from the Old English word *beorg* meaning hill. Turn off the A 51 Chester to Manchester road onto the B5132, not far from Chester at Stamford Bridge. A mile beyond Great Barrow, park close to The Foxcote Inn, a white-painted pub perched on the edge of the slope at Broomhill.

Once known affectionately as 'The Snig' after the Cheshire dialect word for an eel, which in the past were abundant in the nearby Gowy, the pub is still sometimes called  by another of its old names - 'The Railway'. It has been a pub since about 1850, before which it was *"Three dwelling houses with gardens and outbuildings"*. Until 1914 the landlord and his wife would let out spare bedrooms to visitors holidaying in the countryside from Lancashire's industrial towns.

**SJ 469699**   Opposite the pub a rough lane drops downhill between sandstone-walled banks topped with hawthorn. Worn down 12 feet (4 metres) into the bed-rock, the lane is old. Look at the exposed sandstone - in places you can see the aptly named Bunter Pebble Beds made up of pebbles lain down in a river delta 200 million years ago.

20

Because the stone was relatively hard it resisted the later scouring of Ice Age glaciers. This durability also made it popular as a local building stone.

Ahead, the view opens out over the broad flood-plain of the River Gowy. Beyond, the Welsh mountains stretch along the horizon in a pastel backdrop. Away to the R are the storage tanks, tall stacks and orange flares of Stanlow Oil Refinery. Primarily to prevent flood damage to this modern installation, the Gowy's river bed has been substantially lowered and the marshes drained. Now black and white dairy cattle dot the dike-crossed pastures, a dull substitute for reeds and water.

**SJ 468699** The lane snakes downhill. Two hundred metres from the pub a steep flight of stone steps ascends the hedgerow to the L. (It's an alternative route. From the top  of the steps the path skirts the field hedge before turning to the R, downhill towards another stile which rejoins our path). But we go straight on, downhill towards The Hough Farm.

At the bottom of the hill the lane curves into a farmyard fringed with ancient pear trees. In 1838 the tenant, Mr Joseph Brock, was described as, *"a yeoman, farmer and brick and tile maker"*. In those days most country people needed more than one job to make a living.

**SJ 467699** From the farmyard, turn L, into another rough farm track called Ferma Lane, which runs along the contour of the slope towards Great Barrow. Its curious name comes from the Old English *fenn*, mearing fen or marsh. Perhaps the lane ran along the rim of the marsh; a look at the contours seems to confirm this supposition. That the lane is old is supported by the variety of tree species along its length, among them: oak, hawthorn, blackthorn, hazel, ash and elder. A survey of hedges in the parish in 1977 calculated Ferma Lane to be at least 480 years old.

Brambles arc out from the tractor-trimmed hedgerow, while nettles, dock, and tall umbels of cow parsley edge the rutted track. Look out over the first gateway on the R; a line of gnarled fruit trees run down towards the flatter, once marshy ground. The fertile alluvial soil of the river valley has long been recognised; the problem was to drain it. By the early 14th century half a dozen dikes had been built towards Frodsham, and in the 1340s a scheme to build a giant sluice to prevent winter flooding failed when the timbers were swept away by the sea. Reclamation of the marshes was always an expensive business, but after the Black Death had drastically reduced the population work stopped for a while.

**SJ 466697** The lane runs on past a signposted stile up to the L - which is where the alternative route emerges - and then kinks to the R. As it cuts obliquely downhill the surface becomes muddier. When the lane bends to the L again, old but scrawny oak trees shadow the earth. Most of Cheshire's better oaks were cut down during the last two World Wars and never replaced and these feeble specimens are typical of those that remain.

**SJ 463696** A little further on a three-way footpath sign shows three white figures on green grounds marching off in different directions. One continues on Ferma Lane, but we go R, out onto the flat ground of the Gowy Marshes. Centuries ago this was the margin of the mire, where the willows and alders ended and a sea of reeds began. At this point the marshes were half-a-mile (1 km) wide, and stretched across to Mickle Trafford; downstream they were far broader. Imagine the wind soughing across thousands of acres of upright, rafia-hued stems.

A pile of three massive sandstone blocks here may once have been part of a bridge foot or a mill; today they provide a comfortable seat. Cross a crude sleeper bridge over a deep drain and then set out straight across the field, bearing slightly to the L of the distant farm.

**SJ 460697** Past the low concrete parapet of another drainage ditch that runs in from the R, we come to the sluggish River Gowy. It is shallow and rimmed with bur-reeds, rushes, dropwort and yellow flag iris; long fronds pushing up from the silted bottom are stroked out in the current. Though in effect still a 'linear nature reserve' rich with wildlife, today's Gowy is a pale reminder of the ancient river.

Remember the water level was once much higher. A wooden dug-out boat, dating perhaps from the Iron Age, was found in a field near Stamford Bridge in the 1930s. Dredging at the mouth and centuries of land-drainage have reduced the marshes to flat pasture. Only a few willows alongside the old channels give a clue to an older landscape. Ducks and patient herons still use the river and kingfishers nest nearby, but the hosts of water birds are long gone. A last greenshank was killed at Barrowmore in 1890, and a bittern near Tarvin in 1901. Before Stanlow Oil Refinery was built in 1922, flights of noisy geese passed overhead at dusk and dawn.

"*The River Gowy has trout, pikes and eels*", noted a Cheshire naturalist in 1804. Attracted by the fish, otters could at one time be seen along the Gowy and Back Brook. Old accounts agree: "*Otters are occasionally seen at Stamford Bridge.*" (1884); "*Three otters were seen at Stapleford.*" (1892); and, "*Five otters were ruthlessly shot and clubbed to death at Stanney.*" (1902). But you won't see them today.

**SJ 458698** Follow the river, downstream, to the R. Over a stile the cattle-browsed pastures produce pink-gilled mushrooms in late summer and autumn. Before reaching the embankment of the railway line, go L over a farm tractor bridge. From its wooden sleepers look down on the lazy river, where insects and tiny fishes flicker amongst the swaying weeds.

Cross the field to another stile just to the R of the farm buildings. The farmyard is a typical muddle of seed-trays, trailers, harrows and 'Hayters', overlain by the sharp tang of silage and the sweet scent of cattle dung.

**SJ 457698** Go R at the stile. Within 25 metres the thorn-edged farm track meets the railway line at a white, wicket gate. Originally part of the 'Cheshire Lines Committee' railway, trains first reached Chester on this line in 1874. Today a distant two-tone horn warns of the trains' approach, and the tracks weave and undulate away in both directions on their raised embankment across the Gowy Marshes.

**SJ 456701**   Beyond the railway a rough drive bends L and then R, crosses a cattle grid and emerges at a wide turning area in front of St Peter's church, Plemstall.

# St Peter's Church, Plemstall

*Plemstall's ancient parish church stands isolated among chestnuts and black poplars at the end of a lonely lane. Even quite recently it has been cut off by floods, and there is no village and only one farm to share its solitude. Why? - the reason goes back over a thousand years.*

*Tradition says that, sometime during the 7th century, a shipwrecked Irish fisherman vowed that if he was saved he would build a church where he was cast ashore. He landed here, on the 'Isle of Chester', and dedicated his church, naturally, to Peter the fisherman.*

*Two hundred years later, a hermit named Plegmund settled on the Isle, and the place became known as Plemstall, from Plegmondestowe, 'the fenny island of Plegmund.' Plegmund preached at Chester and soon gathered a following. His fame spread, and Alfred the Great called him to his court to help reform the State. A scholar and theologian, he later became Archbishop of Canterbury, and wrote much of the famous Anglo-Saxon Chronicles - the earliest history of any European country in its native language.*

*The church was wholly rebuilt in the 15th century. The wooden belfry was replaced by the present stone tower only in 1826; look carefully and it's easy to trace the outline of the old church. Inside, the church is built without separate nave and chancel, but with two adjoining naves instead. Fragments of medieval glass are preserved in the windows and the church contains a Jacobean three-decker pulpit, much rich carving and several rare Bibles.*

*Amongst the many old tombstones in the churchyard is the 14th*

24

century box tomb of the Hurlestons under the east window. It's carved
with two skeletons (each holding the arrow of Time) one male and one
female - count the ribs!  (Photograph on back cover.)

*Isolated by meadows that were once marshes, the church of St Peter at Plemstall stands on*
*the 'Isle of Chester', close to the River Gowy.*

**SJ  455701**   From  the  churchyard,  if  you've  time,  make  a  short
detour to see Plegmund's Well. Not far down the lane to Mickle Trafford
and  Chester  is  a  bridge  over  Babbins  Brook;  next  to  it  is  Plegmund's
Well. Just discernible in the surrounding stonework is the inscription:

25

> *"Here as in days when Alfred erst was king,*
> *Baptismal water flows from Plegmund's spring."*

**SJ 458700** Return to the church and cross back over the cattle grid. Follow the hawthorn hedge on around the corner; 200 metres later, a sturdy footbridge with stiles at either end spans the Gowy. Look back at the church framed by tall spires of dark yew. Once on the far side, the flatlands of the old marshes open out towards Dunham-on-the-Hill, Bridge Trafford and the Mersey.

From the bridge, cross the fields to a stile beside a ditch and, keeping the drain to your L, continue up the next field. Pick up a handful of the rich, dark alluvial soil. Cold winds cut across these open lands in winter; on old maps this area is aptly called the 'Wild Moors'. Coveys of grey partridges, now declining in Cheshire, burst from beneath the feet in a flurry of wings; and long-billed snipe probe the damp soil in winter, then zig-zag away with a call like tearing cloth.

**SJ 461703** At the top of the field is a junction of weed-choked ditches, crossed by another well-made footbridge. Directly across a further field, go over a stile and turn R, along a broad tractor-access track - called Wildmoor Lane.

The large farm to the L of the track, beyond Barrow Brook, is 200 acre (80 hectares) Morley Hall Farm, bought for £9,000 in 1919. The old Hall stood closer to the railway, but when the farm was burnt down the Hall was rebuilt on the present site. Later, a Spitfire fighter-plane crashed close to the Hall during World War Two.

**SJ 467704** Five hundred metres later, the track skirts the glasshouses and poly-tunnels of Barrow Nurseries who raise 400,000 shrubs annually for the wholesale plant and landscape market: laurels, bamboos, dogwoods, cotoneasters and berberis.

**SJ 468704** Beyond the nurseries, the lane winds on to meet the B5132 below Little Barrow station. Look out over the fields to the L: on

~~~~~~~~~~~~~~~~~~~~~~~~~~~~~~~~~~~~~~~~~~~~~~~~~~~

the horizon is the bulk of Helsby Hill from where an Iron Age fort dominated the heights above the Mersey and the Gowy Marshes.

At the road go R, uphill, past Barrow Lodge and Little Barrow Hall where the outbuildings of the old, working farm are now converted into modern homes. The mid-eighteenth century farmhouse was built from bricks made by next-door-neighbour Joseph Brock, from The Hough. Nearby was the site of Little Barrow quarry, which provided the stone for the re-building of Plemstall church tower in 1826. The stone mason reputedly spent the money he earned on beer, and was said locally, *"to have drunk Plemstall tower"!*

**SJ 469702** Cross the railway bridge. When the railway arrived in 1874 the station soon became busy. Milk was sent to Manchester at 7.30 am every morning; and two-wheeled, iron-tyred milk floats raced to the station from the outlying farms. While, later in the day, trucks of coal were sometimes unloaded for the Manor House in Great Barrow. By 1945 seven trains a day passed through in each direction. Barrow-for-Tarvin station, as it was called, was closed for passengers in 1953.

Beyond the bridge's high-sided parapet, the hill steepens and passes Station Farm, which was the original Little Barrow Hall. Two hundred metres later, on the L, is the Primitive Methodist Chapel, built by public subscription in 1865. For twenty years, from the 1940s, it was a shop; now it's empty.

**SJ 470699** At the top of the hill, 300 feet (100 metres) above sea-level, is the Foxcote Inn once more - a welcome stopping place after the final climb. But before taking refreshment, look back at the spread of the old marshlands below. And picture this hilltop 5,000 years ago, when Stone-Age settlers - one of whose polished stone-axes was found nearby in 1932 - first chose this sandstone outcrop as their home. Surrounded by forest and overlooking a marsh-rimmed sea bay, it must have been a far quieter, bleaker, and more isolated spot than we can properly imagine today.

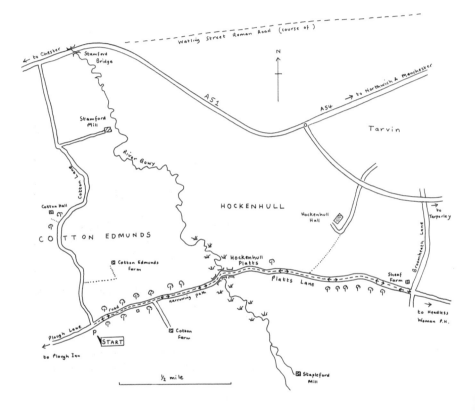

**Hockenhull Platts**

# 2 Hockenhull Platts
## ~ packhorse bridges over the River Gowy ~

Ancient track, sunken lanes, raised causeways across the
marshes, nature reserve and three packhorse bridges.

---

**Start**: *Cotton Edmunds, 3 miles (5 kilometres) east of
Chester. Map reference* **SJ 466654.**
**Distance:** *3 miles (5 kilometres) there and back.*
**Duration:** *3 hours.*
**Maps:** *OS 1:50,000 Landranger Sheet 117 Chester;
OS 1:25,000 Sheet SJ 46.*
**Terrain**: *Virtually flat. Lanes and surfaced paths. Mostly
dry.*
**Food and Drink:** *Pub at either end: Plough Inn, Christleton.
Map reference* **SJ 456652.** *Greenall Whitley. Restricted
opening (Sat all day). Tel: Chester 336096. Or Headless
Woman, Duddon. Map reference* **SJ 511648.** *Greenall
Whitley. Bar snacks and hot meals. Tel: Huxley 252.*

---

It is hard to believe, but for almost 1,400 years after the Romans left
Britain in around AD 410, no proper new roads were built. The Roman
roads, themselves often based on earlier tracks, continued in use
throughout the Middle Ages; but outside the towns they were often
'miry ways', especially in winter.

By the eighteenth century the roads  were in a deplorable condition. The
old system of each parish being responsible for the repair of the roads
within its boundaries had broken down. Deep ruts and floods made the
roads difficult and dangerous to traverse; and there are accounts of
people being drowned in the pot-holes. Defoe in his 1724 'Tour through
Great Britain', states that many roads had become impassable. This, he

adds,

> *"necessarily brought the Country to apply to Parliament; and the consequence has been that Turnpikes or Toll-bars have been set up on the several great Roads of England. Carriages, Droves of Cattle, and Travellers on Horseback are oblig'd to pay an easy Toll, which bears no comparison with the Benefit reap'd thereby".*

Paid for by the tolls, the new roads were a godsend.

But when the new turnpike road from Chester to Nantwich was built in 1743, it by-passed sections of the old London to Holyhead route that had been in use for centuries. Part of this 'lost' road still exists, from Christleton, east of Chester, to Duddon, near Tarporley. It's one of the most interesting sections of medieval roadway left in this country, and certainly the best in Cheshire.

**SJ 463672** Turn off the A51 - the old Roman road - 2 miles (3 kms) east of Chester, down narrow Cotton Lane. It is signposted to 'Cotton Edmunds'. A mile (1.5 kms) later, past Stamford Mill, Cotton Hall, and Cotton Edmunds Farm the lane bends sharp R onto Plough Lane

**SJ 466654** Park near the corner. An unsignposted, narrower, but still metalled lane goes off to the L, overhung with dense ash and oaks. Called Platts Lane, it's a No Through Road, and quiet. Tall cow parsley, purple 'hardheads', and nettles swathe the broad verges. Wood pigeons 'coo' softly in the trees above; and the modern world slips away.

Look out over the gate 50 metres on. To the south Peckforton Castle pokes above the rim of the hills; while to the east Cotton Farm - large, red-bricked and slate-roofed, crouches in a hollow in the fields. Wild cherry, blackthorn, hazel and sycamore grow in the hedgerows. A little farther on and the lane tops a gentle rise and then falls away to the valley of the River Gowy.

~ ~ ~ ~ ~ ~ ~ ~ ~ ~ ~ ~ ~ ~ ~ ~ ~ ~ ~ ~ ~ ~ ~ ~ ~ ~ ~ ~ ~ ~ ~ ~ ~ ~ ~

That this was the old London to Holyhead road is confirmed by Ogilby's 1675 'Britannia Roadbook', which shows the route and mentions the hangman's gibbet that once stood at nearby Brown Heath, a mile (1.5 kms) to the west. The existence of an alternative cart-road to the south - known today as the 'Egg Bridge' route - marked on the map between Boughton and Dutton Hall, suggests that Platts Lane was old even then.

**SJ 469655** Walk on past a footpath that crosses the pastures to the R; it leads off to Guy's Lane and Hargrave. Many of the oak trees here were badly affected by the drought of 1976; their gaunt top branches and secondary crowns bear witness to the lack of water. Out over the fields to the L the distant Mersey's Stanlow oil refinery, with its tall smoke-stacks and gas flare, is visible on the horizon.

**SJ 472656** Beyond a white-gated cottage to the R, hidden behind hedges of lilac and damsons, the road bends to the R, through a gateway to Cotton Farm. Our path runs straight ahead, downhill towards the Gowy. The ditches and verges here are awash with wild flowers and the heady scent of meadowsweet. Narrowing to become a track, the lane slips back another notch into the past.

All sorts of people once came this way, strangers as well as locals. When Celia Fiennes, a Cromwellian colonel's daughter, travelled from Chester to Nantwich during her 'Grand Tour', in 1698, she wrote: "*This is a pretty rich land; you must travel on a causey [causeway] through much wood.*" And, later, she tells how, "*I was engaged by some Highway men; two fellows all of a suddain fell into the road, they look'd truss'd up with great coates and as it were bundles about them which I believe were pistols.*"

Pennant, another inveterate traveller, in his 'Journey from Chester to London', in 1780, also mentions the *'horse road'* from Christleton across Brownheath, by Hockenhull to Tarvin.

While Adam Watkin, in his 'Observations', published in 1791, says that, "*For many ages and to the middle of this [the 18th] century, a causeway about two feet wide with round pebbles was all that man or horse could travel upon ... in Cheshire."*

**SJ 473657** The track, now only a few feet wide, curves on downhill beneath hedges rampant with dog-rose briars. Three hundred metres later, it dwindles to a limestone-gravel surfaced path. Tall willows herald damper soil. A plantation of lofty poplars shiver in the breeze, and head-high reeds, purple loosestrife and water-loving indian balsam crowd the path.

A sandstone-block edged causeway carries the path above the surrounding damp ground. It was once necessary, to lift the road above the Gowy marshes. During its winding 24 mile (38 kms) course the Gowy falls only about 280 feet (90 metres); little enough for a river. From its mouth, where it falls into the Mersey, broad marshes once cut inland past Ince (from the Welsh *ynys* meaning island), Plemstall and Stamford Bridge, as far as Huxley, below the sandstone hills. And so the route to Chester had to be raised above the maze of water, rush and swamp, where sheep graze.

**SJ 456657** This is Hockenhull Platts. The name is old. Its roots are Welsh - from the time when the Gowy was still called the Tarvin river, from the Welsh *terfyn* meaning boundary: that is, on the Welsh marches.

Similarly, the name element *'hock'* may come from the Welsh *hccan* meaning to peddle or sell abroad. *Hen* is the Welsh for 'old'. And *heol* means 'paved way'. While *platts* is an old English word for 'bridges'; a word associated with planks. So Hockenhull Platts means something like 'the bridges on the old peddlars way'.

That the origins of the name date from a period when the Welsh-English boundary was still in what is now Cheshire, back in Anglo-Saxon times, suggests the antiquity of the road itself. It may well pre-date the medieval packhorse bridges by centuries.

~ ~ ~ ~ ~ ~ ~ ~ ~ ~ ~ ~ ~ ~ ~ ~ ~ ~ ~ ~ ~ ~ ~ ~ ~ ~ ~ ~ ~ ~ ~ ~ ~ ~ ~ ~ ~ ~ ~ ~ ~

# Hockenhull Platts ~ Packhorse Bridges

*The three packhorse bridges, sometimes romantically known as the Roman Bridges, were probably built in their present form in the early 14th century. Records show that when the Black Prince passed over them in 1353 he ordered 20 shillings be spent on their repair.*

*The sandstone bridges are joined by causeways, and are as much as 50 metres apart. Each bridge is less than 4 feet wide (1.5 metres), and its parapet is a low 2' 6" (1 metre); while the bridge surface is of mixed cobbles and setts. Some of these are new, but many of the larger stones have evidently been warn smooth by the passage of thousands of hooves and feet, and are old.*

*The bridges came close to destruction in 1824 when the County Council proposed re-routeing the Nantwich to Chester road along Platts Lane. They were saved only the intercession of the Duke of Westminster, on whose land they lay.*

It's a peaceful spot. Dun cattle chew the cud among the aptly named 'Platt Meadows' downstream, while what in the 1860s were 'Home Croft' and 'Well Meadow' is now the 'Cheshire Conservation Trust Hockenhull Platts Nature Reserve. Access By Permit Only'.

Much has changed. Beneath the central bridge the arch footings are raised on an ugly concrete pontoon: the result of a scheme to lower the water level of the whole Gowy, in order to preserve Stanlow oil refinery from flooding. That's progress. Not only have the marshes vanished, but so has a complete habitat that was the haunt of otters as late as the 1880s.

Back in the 17th century Hockenhull Platts was a far wilder place, even if it was on the main road. To stop the surface degenerating into a mire in winter, carts were prevented from using the road by posts set across it at intervals. Macauley, the famous historian, writing of England in 1685, tells us how instead...

*Built in the late Middle Ages to span the Gowy Marshes, the three packhorse bridges at Hockenhull Platts lie on a track that was ancient even then.*

*"Goods were carried by long trains of packhorses. These strong and patient beasts... were attended by a class of men who seem to have born much resemblance to the Spanish muleteers."* The packhorses travelled in convoys of forty or more animals, with the head of each tied to the tail of the one in front. Each convoy was in charge of a *jagger*, or driver, who walked in the lead.

In Cheshire one of the main commodities carried was salt from the Cheshire 'wiches': Northwich, Middlewich and Nantwich, where the natural brine springs have been exploited since prehistoric times.

**SJ 479658** Beyond the three bridges, the path winds uphill again, away from the river. Traces of the old sandstone causeway's edges appear occasionally beside the path. Hazels and dog's mercury in the deep ditch to the R suggest the hedgerow's long history; they are accepted ecological indicators of uninterrupted woodland edge habitat. In places the lane is so worn down - 6-12 feet (2-4 metres) - below the surrounding fields, that it becomes almost a tunnel beneath its blackthorn hedges; and we can imagine the packhorses slipping on the rain-wet stones during a winter descent to the Platts.

**SJ 482657**   Platt lane forks, a third of a mile on, at the top of the slope. The left-hand path goes up Hockenhull Lane to Tarvin. But we continue to the R, on the wider, old road to Duddon. Incongruously, it's now buried under tarmac -, a tacky reminder of misguided 1960s thinking, that detracts from the lane's atmosphere.

Look back over the hedge to the R: the Gowy valley stretches across the foreground; and, beyond, the Welsh hills are dark along the horizon.

**SJ 490655**   Now used mainly by farm tractors, the still sunken lane snakes on beneath ivy-draped oaks. Half a mile (1 km) on, by Sheaf Farm - home to the 'Hockenhull Herefords' - we emerge at Hockenhull crossroads. The farmyard is quiet, and sparrows chatter in the dense holly hedge.

From here there is a choice. Either retrace the outward route and gain a different perspective. Or go on, across the crossroads, and on past the Old Moss, to Duddon Heath and Duddon, where the old packhorse road rejoins the modern A 51 towards the *'passage of Tarporley'*. From there the old road ran on to London.

The old packhorse road across the 'Platts' is little known and quiet; a point emphasised by the steady drum of traffic on the modern main road. Compare the two; and then ask yourself which form of travel you'd prefer - convenience with noise and speed, or a slower progress through rural Cheshire.

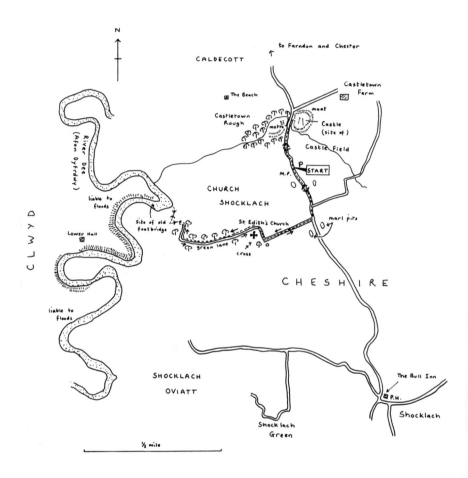

**Shocklach**

# 3 Shocklach ~ *hidden* church on the *Welsh Marches* ~

Norman castle mound, marl pits, isolated church, green lane, ghostly procession and shifting river.

---

**Start**: *Shocklach, 2.5 miles (4 kilometres) south of Farndon. Map Reference* **SJ 436507.**
**Distance:** *2 miles (3 kilometres).*
**Duration:** *2 hours.*
**Maps:** *OS 1:50,000 Landranger Sheet 117 Chester; OS 1:25,000 Sheet SJ 45.*
**Terrain:** *Gentle slope to River Dee. Metalled road; grassy lane, muddy in winter.*
**Food and Drink:** *Bull Inn, Shocklach. Map reference* **SJ 439492.** *Freehouse. Bar snacks and good evening meals. Children welcome. Tel: Tilston 239.*

---

The Welsh-English border has shifted to and fro over the centuries. Today the line follows the natural boundary of the River Dee for a while, between Aldford and Shocklach; on the one side is Cheshire, and on the other Clwyd. But frontiers aren't immutable; they move. Until the seventh century, Cheshire was under Celtic, Welsh control. Just a hundred years later, Anglian settlers from north Germany had pushed the Welsh back into the hills. And by the tenth century the Anglian kingdom of Mercia was 'shired', or sheared, off and became a separate Shire, a forerunner of the Norman county.

Both Wat's Dyke and Offa's Dyke mark the changing fortunes of the Mercian marches west of the Dee, in what is now Wales. While to the east, in Cheshire, the name Tarvin points to an earlier Celtic line - in Welsh *terfyn* means boundary.

From then on, through Norman times and later, the often marshy land on either side of the Dee was to be bandit country. A no-man's-land of castles, cattle raids and uncertainty. If it seems peaceful today, in the past the silence could be misleading, the lull before the storm.

**SJ 436507** Our walk begins a mile (1.5 kms) north of the tiny village of Shocklach, 11 miles (18 kms) south of Chester. From Farndon towards Shocklach, an unclassified road winds south, parallel to the Dee. Just past a roadside sign announcing the village of Shocklach is a lay-by - a good place to park.

Half hidden among the verge-side grasses opposite is a triangular cast-iron mile post. Put up in 1898, it informs us:

<blockquote>
Farndon 3 miles         Chester 11
</blockquote>

and on the other face,

<blockquote>
Shocklach 1         Worthenbury 3
</blockquote>

Back in the 1780s the field opposite was called Brick-kiln Field; a new panorama stretches out beyond the hedge today. Across the fertile valley of the Dee, the white monoliths of Wrexham industrial estate rest against the pastel backdrop of the Welsh hills: Ruabon Mountain and the Clwydian range are blue in the distance. In the past much of the intervening valley was a tangled mossland of marsh, willow and alder. Would our ancestors recognise it now?

**SJ 435508** Keeping to the R of this quiet road, facing any oncoming traffic, walk back towards Farndon for 250 metres. At the entrance to Castletown House Farm, look over the fence to the R.

Here, and deep in the woods opposite, are the still impressive remains of an early Norman castle. After the Conquest, the Normans built scores of minor strongholds to establish local control. Hugh Lupus (the wolf!), Earl of Chester and nephew to William the Conqueror, established a line of castles south-west of Chester at Dodleston,

~~~~~~~~~~~~~~~~~~~~~~~~~~~~~~~~~~~~~~~~~~~~~~~~~~~~~~

Pulford, Aldford, Shocklach, Oldcastle, and Newhall near Combermere. Wood and earth were the materials most easily to hand, and the castles were of the 'motte and bailey' type, such as are shown on the Bayeux Tapestry. The motte was a high mound of earth with a palisade around the top, and the bailey was a courtyard protected by another palisade and a ditch.

At Shocklach, more than 800 years later, the ramparts still stand some 4 metres (12 feet) above the surrounding fields. Ormerod, the Victorian Cheshire historian, tells us the mound was then, " ... *circular, and about twenty feet in perpendicular height"*. Though dry today, the moat was originally fed by the stream that snakes across Castle Field. Imagine the castle as it must once have looked, a statement of Norman power; a fortress in the wilderness.

**SJ 435503** Retrace your steps along the road. A maze of footpaths in the area, testimony to centuries of local use, have since become impassable, or simply vanished. Continue past the lay-by for 300 metres, to the next junction. Here another old road sign, with an octagonal post and an ornamental ball-shaped top, points on towards Shocklach. Shortly afterwards, 30 metres on, an unmarked narrow metalled lane goes downhill to the R.

The numerous small ponds alongside the road are marl pits where specialist contractors dug out marl, a limy clay once used as a kind of primitive fertiliser. Now cattle drink at their bullrush-choked edges.

**SJ 432501** Open to breezes from the Welsh hills, the lane slopes gently down towards the river. At the bottom is an ivy-clad, brick-built shed with an old, bench-seated privy at the rear. The lane bends R. A few yards on, nestling among conifers and tall horse chestnuts, is the little known Norman church of St. Edith's, Shocklach.

Enter the churchyard through the wooden kissing-gate. Here, tall Victorian tombstones mingle with solid box tombs, most with dates from the 1800s; but half hidden in the turf below the east window is a recumbent slab with the barely visible date of 1664. At the turn of the century the old custom of strewing the graves with rushes at certain times of year was still observed at this out of the way place.

On the L of the path, opposite the beautiful Norman carved doorway, is an ancient octagonal cross shaft remounted on a later plinth. Still in its original position on the south side of the church, the cross has a significant history. Church crosses were where labourers were hired each year by the local farmers, where payments were made, where pedlars sold their wares, and where parish matters were settled.

Shocklach cross was also used as a plague stone. Epidemics swept Cheshire several times in the 16th and 17th centuries and, even in this quiet corner, families and whole communities were devastated. But life must go on; and in around 1600 the cross shaft was used as a market place. Look on the top: the four fist-sized depressions in the stone were once filled with vinegar to disinfect coins, and business was conducted at what they hoped was a safe distance.

*One of the best examples in Cheshire, the fine twelfth century south doorway at Shocklach shows the characteristic Norman cable and chevron, or zig-zag, carving.*

# Saint Edith's Church, Shocklach

*St. Edith's church, Shocklach, was built in about 1150 by the lord of the manor, Thomas de Shocklach (who lived in the castle), to serve the three townships of Caldecott, Church Shocklach and Shocklach Oviatt. It is dedicated to St. Edith of Polesworth, one of the sisters of the Saxon King Edward the Elder. Edith means 'the blessed'. Many maps fail to show the church; and looking at them one can only guess at the church's site by the meeting of ancient footpaths.*

*'Socheliche' is how the name appears in the Domesday Book. 'Lache' meant mire or slutch. So Shocklach comes out as just another muddy-sounding form of 'such slutch', or something close. An indication of the church's long isolation is scratched with a diamond ring upon the east window, by travellers taking overnight sanctuary: "I Robt. Aldersley was here the 31st day of October 1756 along with John Massie and Mr Derbyshire. NB. The roads were so bad we were in danger of our lives."*

*Built of irregular sandstone blocks, the church is small and simple. The only exterior refinement is the fine Norman south doorway, with its typical round-headed entrance carved with chevrons (zig-zags) and rope-like cables. The double bellcote houses a pair of bells which were originally rung from outside. (Two sets of bells have been stolen in recent years, and the church is now protected by a flashing light and an ear-piercing electronic intruder alarm).*

*Inside the church - which can be viewed at 48 hours notice to the church-wardens - are a 15th century font, late 17th century pews and pulpit, 18th century altar rails, and two Elizabethan sanctuary chairs. While carved into the stone in the north-west corner, is a recently re-discovered relief of a mounted medieval knight in armour.*

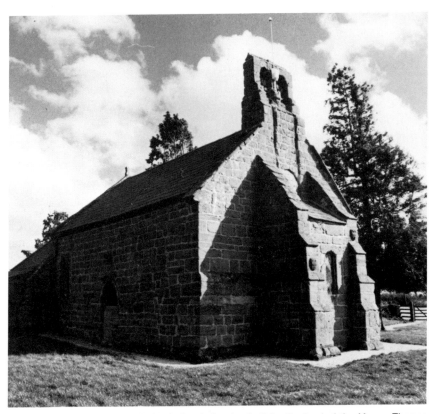

*Viewed from the west, Shocklach's isolated church - built by the Lord of the Manor, Thomas de Shocklach, in about AD 1150 - is dominated by a curious double bellcote.*

Out in the lane once more, go L and L again as the now grassy track runs on down towards the river. Rutted by winter tractors, this green lane sees other, more ghostly wheels pass each night. For, so the story goes, the Breretons, Barons of Malpas, some on horseback and some in coaches, come this way in the darkness in a long and opulent procession to view their old domain. And, at midnight they stop and climb down outside their remote, unspoilt church.

42

~~~~~~~~~~~~~~~~~~~~~~~~~~~~~~~~~~~~~~~~~~~~~~~~~~~~~

**SJ 432502** Still alongside the churchyard, a sturdy stile leads off to the R; but after a quarter of a mile (0.5 km) the path peters out, like most around here. So, instead, we follow the lane on downhill. The soil turns from dry sand to cloying clay. Purple loosestrife, lilac vetches, nettles and dog roses decorate the tree fringed path. Gnarled hawthorns draped in briars loom over the now sunken lane, 1 metre (3 feet) below the surrounding fields - testimony to its age. The number of tree varieties, too, are a clue to the lane's antiquity: ash, oak, elder, alder, hazel, hawthorn, blackthorn, crab apple, wild briar, ivy, and the rarer tooth-leaved wild service tree; all of them have sown themselves here over the centuries.

**SJ 427502** At the bottom of the lane, half a mile (1 km) away over a gate, you can see three-storeyed, brick built Lower Hall; across the looping Dee, it's in another country - Wales. Close to the river now, our path jinks sharply R. It's almost overgrown with water loving plants: sedges, columbine and blue forget-me-nots. Sixty metres on, a gate beneath tall ashes marks the end of the lane. Perhaps it once continued to the river's banks.

From here it's possible to trace the shifting paths that once took villagers and farm workers across the fields alongside the river. Many are marked on old maps; and there are still numerous rights of way in the area. But all traces of these vanished routes have now been engulfed by ragged grass and nettles. Close use of the 1:25,000 map is to be advised. A hundred metres diagonally out from the gate a low, stone farm bridge crosses a deep drainage ditch. Beyond, three successive wide gulleys are the last vestiges of old loops of the river. Now solid and overgrown, they lead to the water's edge. Here the Dee is still scouring at its sandy banks, cutting out yet another future loop. A map of 1874 shows an island here. A little upstream there used to be a footbridge that crossed over into Wales; and, until the 1950s, there was a Ferry Cottage too.

What a shame they've gone; instead we must return the way we came, back through history, to our cars and roads and fast-paced lives.

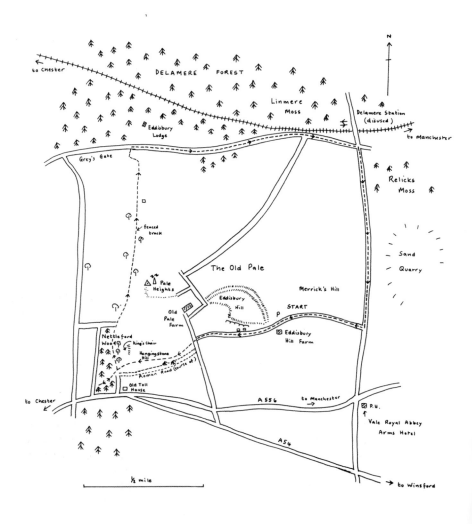

**Delamere**

EXTEND USING DELAMERE FOREST

# 4 Delamere ~ along Watling Street
## below the hillfort ~

Iron Age and Saxon hillfort, Roman road, medieval quarry and round the 'Old Pale'.

**Start**: *Eddisbury Hill, near Kelsall. Map reference* **SJ 556692.**
**Distance:** *4.5 miles (7 kilometres).*
**Duration:** *3 hours.*
**Maps:** *OS 1:50,000 Landranger Sheet 117 Chester; OS 1:25,000 Sheet SJ 56 and 57.*
**Terrain:** *Undulating upland. Lanes, field edges, forestry tracks, roadside. One steep climb. Usually dry.*
**Food and Drink:** *The Vale Royal Abbey Arms Hotel, Chester Road, Oakmere. Map reference* **SJ 563686.** *Greenall Whitley. Bar snacks and hot meals. Restaurant. Tel: Sandiway 882747.*

Iron Age Cheshire - in the five centuries before the Romans came - was not the untouched wilderness we might suppose. A line of hillforts along Cheshire's central sandstone ridge marked what, even then, was a far earlier trade route; one that had already seen Neolithic polished stone axes from the axe-factories of north Wales, and gold from Ireland, pass north to south along it for two thousand years. There were other routes too, from the brine springs at what are now Northwich, Middlewich and Nantwich, that crossed the Cheshire Plain from east to west. By the Iron Age both tracks were long established.

There were far fewer people then, of course. But for centuries Celtic Iron Age tribes had loved, quarrelled, eaten, slept and died in Cheshire. The Deceangli to the west, and the Cornovii to the east, were nomadic

45

pastoralists whose flocks ranged over the drier uplands. When they settled, it was to cultivate small square fields cleared from the still extensive woodlands. And to protect themselves, during a period of climatic decline and already increasing population, they built hillforts.

Eddisbury hillfort, near Delamere, stands close to a probable prehistoric crossroads, at a meeting of two ancient tracks. It's one of history's focal points; and where our walk begins.

**SJ 563686**  Turn off the A556 Chester to Manchester road at the bottom of Kelsall Hill, opposite The Vale Royal Abbey Arms Hotel. Chester is 9 miles (15 kms) away, and Manchester 30 miles (48 kms). The road is signposted as the B5152 to Frodsham. Within a third-of-a-mile (0.5 km), turn L up steep Eddisbury Hill. Park on the verge just before the top, close to Eddisbury Hill Farm on the L.

**SJ 555692**  From high on Eddisbury Hill - a flat-topped plateau of Keuper sandstone, covered with 2-3 feet (1 metre) of glacial drift - the view encompasses the dark swathes of ancient Delamere Forest. Now clad in conifers, the forest was once heath and mixed oak-woodland. The forest soil is sand and gravel and, though poor, is light, well-drained and easy to till. This attracted  Bronze Age settlers, long before the fort was built. Theirs are the seven tumuli - or burial mounds, one mile (1.5 kms) south-east of Eddisbury, at Seven Lows Farm. There are many others, too, in and around the forest: Coblow, Roughlow, Oulton Low, Hounslow, Rulow, Garraslow, Kelsbarrow, Willow Wood, and Wanslow Well. Sadly, most have disappeared, ploughed out by centuries of agriculture.

Five wedge-shaped neolithic stone hammers were found at the foot of Eddisbury Hill in 1896. And in 1851 a Bronze Age burial urn containing burnt human bones was discovered close to the Roman road, about half-a-mile (1 km) from Eddisbury Hill Farm. According to the Victorian finder, one of the stones covering the urn was large and, "*like a human bust*".

*Overlooking the Cheshire Plain, the northern ramparts of what the Anglo-Saxon Chronicles called Eades' Byrig overlie a far older Iron Age hillfort.*

Opposite the farm rise the ramparts of Iron Age Eddisbury hillfort, its steep grass-covered slopes topped with gorse and hawthorn. It is the largest and undoubtedly the most complex Iron Age site in Cheshire. Unfortunately, though, it's on private ground; if you want to look at the overgrown defences, then ask for permission. The land belongs to Eddisbury Hill Farm.

**SJ 554692** A little-used private lane climbs round the back of the hill. The tall grass at the top used to be a favourite spot for courting couples; in summer now, it's a dense jungle of nettles and purple rosebay willowherb.

# Eddisbury Iron Age Hillfort

*Eddisbury hillfort was built initially in the Iron Age - hundreds of years before the arrival of the Romans - to guard the route through the Kelsall Gap. It has a long history of both legendary and proved use.*

*When the fort was excavated by Liverpool University in 1935-38, they found two distinct prehistoric phases. Research showed that, at first, a single bank and ditch enclosed only the eastern end of the hill. Later on, the fort was enlarged to take in the whole of the hill top; an area roughly the same as the large field we see today. The first stage rampart and ditch were buried under the edges of the new defences, and were only discovered during excavation.*

*When the Romans arrived, they quickly overran most British hillforts using arrow-firing artillery and disciplined siege tactics. At Eddisbury, the palisades and earth ramparts were thrown down, and the ditches levelled. The Romans may have used the hill as a signal station, but otherwise Eddisbury remained a deserted ruin for the next 800 years.*

*Long after the Romans had left Britain, the fort was rebuilt in around AD 915, by Aethelflaeda, the daughter of Alfred the Great. At the same time her husband, Ethelred, re-fortified Chester. Both were to protect Cheshire against the Danes. New ramparts were built over the Iron Age remains, and new ditches cut. It is these massive earthworks - which still tower 18 feet (6 metres) above the silted-up ditch, that we can see today as a double line of defences to the east and north. The name Eddisbury is Anglo-Saxon and comes from* Eades' Byrig, *which means the fort belonging to Eade - its commander, perhaps.*

From the hillfort a narrow country lane runs on downhill past aptly named 'Old Pale' and 'Eddisbury Hill' cottages. It was still a farm track as late as the 1930s. Beyond the hedge on the R, fields of wheat and pasture rise to the outcropping sandstone sill that formed a natural base for part of the hillfort.

~~~~~~~~~~~~~~~~~~~~~~~~~~~~~~~~~~~~~~~~~~~~~~~~~~~

**SJ 552691** Four hundred metres later, the road bends L, on Stoney Lane, once more prosaically known as Eddisbury Road, down towards the A556. Continue through the gate, straight on, on the signposted footpath.

We're now almost on the line of the Manchester (Mamucium) to Chester (Deva) Roman road called Watling Street. From Northwich (Condate), to the east, the road climbed beneath the fort on Eddisbury Hill, and then followed the contours along the slope of the high ground, towards Chester. In the past the lower ground here was damper and even swampy, as the local names on old maps suggest - nearby are Plovers Moss, Thieves Moss and Riley Moss - obliging the Roman engineers to keep to the tops. From the gate, the Roman road ran perhaps 50 metres down the hill, parallel to our path. In Victorian times, a section of the road was discovered here in a spinney above the school; but, like many archaeological relics, it has since succumbed to modern mechanised agriculture.

It's easy to forget that until the new turnpike road from Northwich to Chester was built in 1769, this was not just the old road, but the only road. During the Jacobite Rebellion in 1745, a trench was dug across the road near here to obstruct the southern march of Bonnie Prince Charlie's troops. The path follows the field edge towards a group of Scots pines. With the modern road, the A 556, out of sight below, the open fields evoke an impression of space and an older, wilder landscape.

**SJ 549689** The stand of Scots pines, by the hedge 350 metres on, holds a remnant of what has been described, rather grandly, as *"the most remarkable section of a Roman road in Britain."* It's an optimistic appraisal. But in the rough grass is a 10 feet (3 metres) deep hollow cut into a brow of the hill. Here in 1885, the Victorian author of 'Roman Cheshire', W.T. Watkin, made an exploratory excavation. He found a 36 feet (11 metres) wide cutting with a 10 feet (3 metres) wide roadway in the middle. Worn 10 inches (25 cms) into the rock were the wheel ruts of carts; exactly 4' 6" (1.5 metres) apart, they were identical in gauge to those on the Roman road over Blackstone Edge, east of Manchester.

A section of Roman Watling Street exposed near Eddisbury hillfort, showing the single carriageway with wheel ruts 1.4 metres (4'6") apart and a central groove gouged probably by carts' brakes. (Photograph courtesy of Canon M.H.Ridgway.)

Here, too, is a curious forked oak tree which has grown round a large rock jammed between the two trunks, and suspended 18 inches off the ground.

**SJ 547689** A hundred metres on, beyond a stile, the route of the Roman road follows the hedge-line for a while, beneath a clump of oaks and pines. As the dotted line on the Ordnance Survey map shows, far more of the road across Organsdale Field was once visible. But what disuse began, the plough has completed. The raised agger that carried the metalled surface has long since disappeared; though the *fossae,* or

50

~~~~~~~~~~~~~~~~~~~~~~~~~~~~~~~~~~~~~~~~~~~~~~~~~~~

ditches, were still detectable in Victorian times. A few stones are all that remain today, cleared from the soil, and heaped among the ragweed, thistles and knotgrass along the boundary to the R.

**SJ 541688** At the field before the forest edge, climb over the stile and go L, down the fence. Here, on the lip of the slope, the route of the Roman road becomes visible once more as a broad platform cut into the hill. As the road leaves Organsdale Field, there are the vestiges of a bank on either side. On towards the forest edge, a sandstone outcrop has been cut back to allow the road to pass; and the road follows the contour of the slope into the trees. Now look back, and trace a straight line across the fields to the distant clump of pines. Imagine the road; and imagine, too, the thousands of people who have passed this way over the centuries: ancient celts, Roman legionaries, carters taking stone to build medieval Vale Royal Abbey, drovers and soldiers, labourers and lords, foot travellers and horsemen.

**SJ 540689** Return to the top of the slope and climb over a stile into the trees. Soon the bracken fringed path meets, at right angles, a wider forestry track rising from the main road. On the other side, the Roman road can be traced still, as it runs on down towards Kelsall. When excavated, a 10 feet (3 metres) deep, and 36 feet (12 metres) wide channel was found cut into the rock. Traces of the banks on either side can be seen among the trees.

**SJ 538688** Here too, is a fork in the Roman road, the parting of the ways for Manchester and Middlewich; a place once known as 'Hinds Well'. (See the 1:25,000 map). The Middlewich (Salinis) road lines up with a toll cottage on the A 556, and merges with the modern road to Winsford (at the modern junction!) about half-a-mile (1 km) away. A lesser road, it was only 30 feet (10 metres) wide.

**SJ 539689** Now return to the broad, sandy forestry track; it's part of the Sandstone Trail. Go L, up the hill, away from the road. On the R, at the top of a slope, are the shallow quarries of Kings Chair, reputed to have been the source of building stone for Vale Royal Abbey, in 1277-1300. Tall oaks and silver-trunked beeches shade the path and, in

~~~~~~~~~~~~~~~~~~~~~~~~~~~~~~~~~~~~~~~~~~~~~~~~~~~~~~~

places where the air is still, a sweet, resinous scent rises from the sun-warmed pines.

From here we circle the 'Old Pale', a hill enclosed from Delamere Forest in 1338, under the orders of Edward III, "*to make a chamber in the forest for the preservation of vert and venison.*" The pale was a fence to protect deer. The head forester's house, known as the 'chamber in the forest', once stood close to Iron Age Eddisbury hillfort.

Continue straight on along the forestry track, keeping the edge of the forest and Hangingstone Hill, with its sandstone outcrops, to the R.

**SJ 540697** At the end of Nettleford Wood (*fford* is the Celtic Welsh for way or road - a clue to the nearby presence of the Roman road), half-a-mile (1 km) later, the path enters open country. A sign on the gate warns, *'Sheep and Lambs. Dogs must be kept on leads'*. On top of the hill, to the R, are a group of police and civil defence aerials above a new bunker: a modern facet of mysterious Cheshire.

Beneath an avenue of tall sycamores, the path runs downhill for another half-a-mile (1km), past white-painted Eddisbury Lodge Cottage. Here and there, forbidding show-jumps for horses interrupt the sheep fencing. This is a lovely stretch at any season, with distant views over the forest to the west and north.

**SJ 540704** At the bottom the path comes to a crossroads. Across a limestone-surfaced road the sign points on to private Eddisbury Lodge Farm. We go R, towards 'Linmere Car Park and Delamere Stn'.

The rough road winds along the forest edge; where horses flick their tails at flies beneath the trees, and wood pigeons 'coo' softly from the dappled shade.

**SJ 546704** Where the forest closes in on either side, another half-a-mile (1 km) on, the Forestry Commission have planted a small arboretum - a collection of trees. As a numbered plaque explains, there are only 33 truly native trees in Britain, among the 1,500 or so that

~~~~~~~~~~~~~~~~~~~~~~~~~~~~~~~~~~~~~~~~~~~~~~~~~~~~~~

grow here. Among them, here, see if you can identify: rowan, ash, birch, alder, elder, hornbeam, holly, willow, sycamore, wild cherry, and sessile and pedunculate oaks.

**SJ 548704**   On again, we come to the Forestry Commission's 'Old Pale Nursery' and 'Polyhouse Unit'. Of the 2,500 acres (900 hectares) of forest, about 125 acres (50 hectares), including some at Abbot's Moss, are tree nursery, where they grow 7-8 million trees a year. Nearby is a visitor centre; well worth a tour, it explains the history of the forest, and shows how it is managed today.

From the visitor centre, the now metalled road runs alongside the twin-tracked Chester to Manchester railway-line, until it meets Station Road, the busy B 5152 Frodsham to Tarporley road, at Delamere Station.

**SJ 556702**   Cross over to the footpath on the B 5152, and turn R, back towards Eddisbury Hill. On the L, screened by trees, is the Marley Tiles works and quarry where glacial sands are extracted. A Warrington to Middlewich (Mediolano) Roman road, suggested by Cheshire historians, must have come somewhere close to the modern straight road; but there is no evidence today. Cattle graze placidly on one side of the busy road, and there are prim houses on the other. Three quarters of a mile (1.2 km) later, turn R, back up Eddisbury Hill. But first, look out over the field to the L, towards an arm of the forest; until recently the raised agger of the Roman road could be seen curving across the grassland until it disappeared into the trees.

**SJ 561692**   As you slog up steep Eddisbury Hill lane, back towards the car, think how the Roman legionaries must have felt as they climbed the same sharp slope: they had probably already marched from Condate (Northwich). And now, *by Jupiter!* they had to walk on to Deva (Chester). Are not the gods unkind?

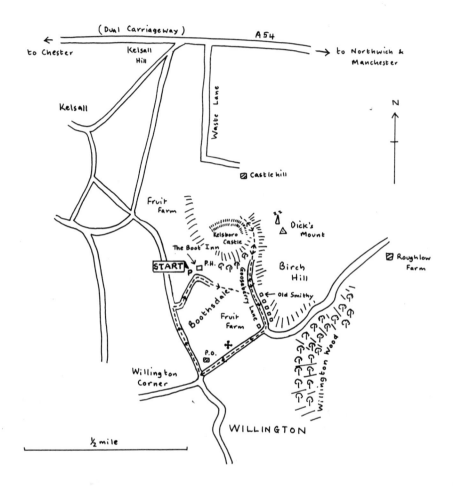

**Willington**

# 5 Willington ~ *above 'Little Switzerland'* ~

**Hidden valley, sheltered fruit farms, shelf-like path, Iron Age hillfort and pleasant views.**

---

**Start:** *Willington, 1 mile (0.5 kilometre) south of Kelsall. Map reference* **SJ 530673.**

**Distance:** *1.5 miles (2.5 kilometres).*

**Duration:** *2 hours.*

**Maps:** *OS 1:50,000 Landranger sheet 117 Chester; OS 1:25,000 SJ 56 and 57.*

**Terrain:** *Gentle climb to top of Boothsdale. Lanes, sandy footpaths, quiet roadside. Dry.*

**Food and Drink:** *The Boot Inn, Boothsdale, Willington. Map reference* **SJ 530673.** *Greenall Whitley. Open every lunchtime and evenings. Bar snacks. Restaurant. Tel: Kelsall 51375.*

---

"*Willington*," so 'Kelly's Directory of Cheshire' for 1912 tells us, "*is a parish 3.5 miles south from Mouldsworth Station ....*" At first glance, this seems an odd way to start a summary of a place. But there is a good reason. When the Cheshire Lines railway from Manchester to Chester opened in the 1840s, the city's crowded workers were keen to escape into the countryside on the train - for cars had yet to come - and Willington seized its opportunity. Until the First World War, Willington was known as 'Little Switzerland'; and the first 'tourists' came to stay in local cottages, to climb the hills, to walk in the quiet lanes and to take a breath of Cheshire air. Looking back from an age of package holidays it seems a quaint idea; but then much has changed - in both Willington and the world.

**SJ 530673** Today, our approach to 'Little Switzerland' begins at The Boot Inn, at the bottom of Boothsdale, in Willington. Turn off the A 54 Kelsall by-pass at the top of the hill, and dropping down through the now peaceful village on the old main road, turn down  by the foot-bridge at the sign for Willington. Half-a-mile (1 km) along Willington Road, turn L immediately after a dip; if you come to Willington Corner or Willington Hall, you've gone too far. It's easy to miss. So keep your eyes peeled for the large green notice for 'The Boot Inn' and the road-sign for 'Boothsdale'. After all, many of the best places are those that are the most difficult to find; and its hidden position adds to its charm.

The Boot Inn, with its large car park, was once a row of small cottages, in brick and sandstone. It is now an attractive, low ceilinged, stone floored pub, with crudely-made tables of oak outside. The tree-clad slope rises steeply behind; and a cockerel crows in the garden. An earlier landlord was one of the last working thatchers in the county, in the days when most country people had more than one job. The pub was known previously as 'Joe Lloyd's' or 'The Cat'; the latter an unpleasant reminder of a distant occasion when a live cat was thrown onto the fire for a bet! Romantic notions of life in the past being a rural idyll are sometimes misplaced; and hopefully, we are more civilised today.

Beyond the pub, continue on along lilac-hedged Cat Lane. The tiny, brick and sandstone cottage on the R is, for the moment at least, a reminder of the simple cottages of the area in the past. There are horses in the fields, and the silence is punctuated only by small noises. Together they evoke a past before the coming of the 'infernal' combustion engine and the motor car.

**SJ 531672** A hundred metres on, the lane forks. To the L a sign announces 'Private Road, Boothsdale House, Farm and Cottage'. Take the right-hand fork, straight on, signposted for lovely-sounding 'Gooseberry Lane'. Soon the track curves R, into the sheltered fields of a fruit farm. But we go L, straight on between two posts and up a narrow footpath. The tall, overhanging hedges here form a long, green, ascending tunnel, dappled with shade in the summer sun. In spring the sandy path is white with the fallen blossoms of the wayside may, like

~~~~~~~~~~~~~~~~~~~~~~~~~~~~~~~~~~~~~~~~~~~~~~~~~~~~~~~~

some confetti-covered church path.

**SJ 533672** At the top of the slope the path emerges into the open again, on Gooseberry Lane. The name is older than the fruit farms, which were started only after World War Two, and its origin is obscure. Turn L, on up the hill, signposted for 'Kelsall'. Many of the cottages perched on the steep bank date from the 1860s; and even in 1911, the population of Willington as a whole was still only 139. Even so, the cottagers were quick to seize the opportunity of a second income and, according to the oldest resident of Gooseberry Lane, *"the cottages would clear a bedroom out"*, and offer bed and breakfast to visitors who arrived from the station in horse-drawn carts.

As the lane climbs, the view opens out to the L, and the name 'Little Switzerland' takes on a clearer meaning. If large-eyed dun cattle with bells around their necks ambled across the steep flower-spangled meadows, it wouldn't be surprising.

**SJ 533673** As the lane peters out towards the last house high on the bank, a wooden signpost points off to the L along a curious raised path that skirts the contours of the slope. Its age is uncertain. But the drystone walls on either side, one dropping away, and the other holding back the hillside, make it perhaps unique in Cheshire. Green flowered pennywort and the purple spires of foxgloves decorate the crevices. And, where the sweeping branches of horse chestnuts arch over the path, it's like being on a high natural verandah, perched over Boothsdale.

Families of grey squirrels live in tangled dreys in the tall beech trees that dominate the slopes of Birch Hill, up to the R. You may also hear the high, laughing cry of the elusive green woodpecker somewhere in the trees above. Or the soothing 'coos' of woodpigeons hidden among the leaves.

**SJ 533674** Close to the top, stop on the bend of the path and look back. The view has changed little since the first visitors from Manchester gazed out over the Cheshire Plain from here a generation ago. In the foreground, a few typical Cheshire cottages shelter in the deep combe of Boothsdale. The dark shelter belts of tall conifers are relatively new, but the green chequer-board of fields beyond would be familiar to anyone sitting here at the turn of the century. The Peckforton and Bickerton hills stretch away to the L, with the outlying wedge of Harthill jutting out towards Wales. Close to the Dee you can see Eaton Hall too - the home of the Duke of Westminster - once a Victorian palace, but since replaced by a modern monstrosity and, "*all lights now*".

**SJ 533675** At the top a stile climbs through a gap in the trees and out into open pasture. It's a different world. The sturdy three-barred fences here are a last relic of the days when Castle Hill was a stud farm for prize shire horses. At a cost of between £3. 10s (£3.50) and 6 guineas (£6.30) the stallions were taken out to sire foals as far away as the Wirral, Chester and Helsby.

While, during World War Two, the RAF communications aerial up on Dick's Mount to the R, meant local people had to be especially vigilant over the black out; a light here could be seen from Wales and, for fear of being bombed or strafed, "*you mustn't even strike a match*".

A standing stone in the fields here, known as the 'Whipping Stone', was removed during the last century. Local opinion suggests it marked the site of a prize stallion's grave.

**SJ 532675** Most interesting though, are the traces of Iron Age Kelsborrow Castle, visible as a steep encircling bank and ditch in the pasture to the L.

# Kelsborrow Castle

*An oval Iron Age promontory-fort, Kelsborrow Castle takes advantage
of the natural headland created by Boothsdale on the south-east and the
steep scarp on the west. Although there is higher ground to the east,
the 400 feet (125 metres) high site is easily defensible. Centuries of
ploughing have spread the soil of the ramparts that curve around the
north side of the 7 acre (3 hectares) enclosure. Even so, the earthwork
banks still rise up to 6 feet (2 metres) above the bottom of the outer
ditch. Over 100 feet (30 metres) wide, the defences were obviously
formidable; and were almost certainly once topped by a wooden
palisade. There is no sign of an entrance along the length of the
rampart, and it seems probable that, as elsewhere, access was along
the edge of the slope, at the Boothsdale end.*

*Kelsborrow was the home of people of the peace-loving Cornovii tribe,
who were later easily subdued by the Romans. Traces of small Celtic
fields have been found to the north, in Kelsall, while the area carries
numerous clues - in the shape of flint tools, to long occupation by people
long before the Iron Age.*

*Though so far unexcavated, the site yielded a 6 inches (15 cms) long
bronze axe-head in 1810 and, later, a piece of an iron sword. It's a
protected monument, and on private ground, so no digging is allowed!*

Though the path continues past Castle Hill Farm to Quarry Bank Lane,
we return over the stile and back down Boothsdale. In late summer huge
dragonflies patrol the edge of the trees on the lookout for insect prey.
Parties of Iron Age women may have descended the hill by the same
route in the early morning to fetch water from springs at the bottom of
the hill. And, much later, we can imagine shire horses plodding
carefully down Boothsdale, led by a man or boy in front, on their way
to be shod at the blacksmith's.

**SJ 533673** At the bottom of the narrow path, continue on down
Gooseberry Lane. Go on, past the path back to the Boot Inn. One of the

now ostentatiously refurbished cottages here was the old smithy, built in 1861. Later, a van came out twice a week from Nantwich to supply the local people with groceries.

*A chestnut mare grazes peacefully beside the hanging path that climbs Boothsdale to the Iron Age hillfort of Kelsborrow Castle..*

~~~~~~~~~~~~~~~~~~~~~~~~~~~~~~~~~~~~~~~~~~~~~~~~~~~~~~

**SJ 534670** Soon the lane curves beneath damson and cherry trees to emerge on Chapel Lane. Turn R, downhill. On the corner here is, 'Winsor's Willington Fruit Farm', which sells, 'Apples and other Fruits in Season'. Clever siting on the slopes of Willington Hill assures the fruit is above the early and late frost levels; while shelter belts of tall conifers protect the vulnerable buds and flowers from the prevailing westerly winds. At different times of the year you can buy: apples, strawberries, rhubarb, blackcurrants, broad and runner beans.

**SJ 532669** Downhill, 150 metres later, on the R, is the old United Methodist chapel, built in 1823. It's now a smart house.

A little further on, look into the tiny fields sheltered by 25 feet (8 metres) high clipped conifer hedges. Full of umbrella-sized rhubarb leaves, they are like the tall green rooms of some ancient roofless palace, open to the air and illuminated by the sun.

**SJ 531667** Where Chapel Lane meets Willington Road, at the bottom of the hill, is the village post office on the corner. A previous postmaster remembers his mother selling postcards of 'Little Switzerland' here to visitors before the First World War.

Cross the road onto the footpath, and turn R, back towards Kelsall. Willington Road is still quiet, with mixed new and older, converted cottages and farmhouses on either side.

**SJ 529671** A quarter-of-a-mile (0.5 km) later, turn R, back up Boothsdale, to the Boot. Damson trees still dot the hedges here as in much of older Cheshire. On foot it's easier to get the measure of the place: there's the white house at the top of Gooseberry Lane; there's the radio aerial that guided planes during the war; and there's the far older hillfort called Kelsborrow Castle at the top of Boothsdale. And there's the Boot Inn.

All that history can make you thirsty.

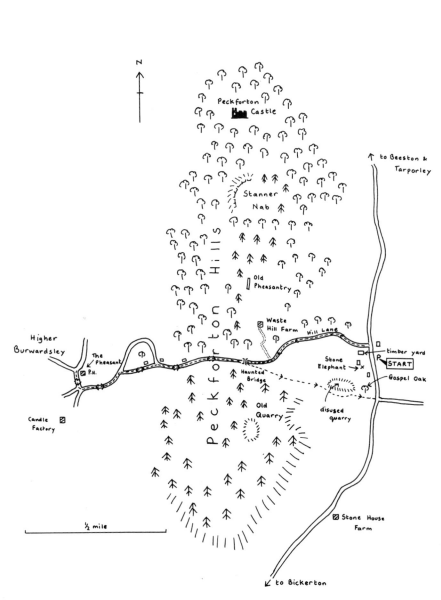

N

to Beeston &
Tarporley

Peckforton
Castle

Stanner
Nab

P e c k f o r t o n   H i l l s

Old
Pheasantry

Waste
Hill Farm    Hill Lane

Higher
Burwardsley

The
Pheasant

P.H.

Stone
Elephant

timber yard

P
START

Haunted
Bridge

Gospel Oak

disused
quarry

Candle
Factory

Old
Quarry

½ mile

Stone House
Farm

to Bickerton

**Peckforton**

# 6 Peckforton ~ *from the Stone*
## *Elephant to The Pheasant* ~

**Cheshire's own elephant and castle, cobbled estate track, saltway over the hills, haunted bridge, panoramic views and a Gospel Oak.**

---

**Start:** *Peckforton, 4 miles (6.5 kilometres) south-west of Tarporley. Map reference* **SJ 538566**.
**Distance**: *3 miles (5 kilometres).*
**Duration**: *2 hours.*
**Maps**: *OS 1:50,000 Landranger Sheet 117 Chester; OS 1:25,000 SJ 55.*
**Terrain**: *Steady climb to ridge. Cobbled estate track, sandy lane and rough pasture. Usually dry.*
**Food and Drink**: *The Pheasant Inn, Higher Burwardsley. Map reference* **SJ 523566**. *Free House. Hot and cold food every day. Tel: Tattenhall 70434*

---

At Peckforton, beneath the shadow of Cheshire's wooded central sandstone ridge, two rivers begin within a stone's throw of each other. While the Weaver snakes south before looping north just inside the Cheshire-Shropshire border near Audlem, the tiny, less well known Gowy meanders north for 19 miles (30 kms), past Beeston Castle, to flow into the Mersey.

The cradle of both streams is Peckforton Moss - once a swampy wasteland, but now open farmland, much of it reclaimed since the 1840s. Between the Moss and the hills lies the picturesque village of Peckforton with its tiny black and white cottages, some of which date from the 16th century.

**SJ 538566** Our walk begins just over a mile (2kms) from the A49, close to the centre of Peckforton village. Park on the wide verge opposite the end of Hill Lane. Until the mid-1800s the village had almost twice the number of houses it does today; in 1841 there were 61, compared to only 34 today. Many of the scattered black and white cottages are thatched; look for the reed finials on two rooves - they're crafted in the shape of pheasants.

Close to the village centre, and next to the saw mill, is Laundry Cottage. Behind its neat holly hedge, silhouetted among the bright flowers, is one of Cheshire's most unusual oddities: a 12 feet (4 metres) high stone elephant with a castle on its back.

*Cheshire's own elephant and castle was carved in 1859 by John Watson, stonemason to Peckforton Castle.*

64

~~~~~~~~~~~~~~~~~~~~~~~~~~~~~~~~~~~~~~~~~~~~~~~~~~~~~~

# The Peckforton Stone Elephant

*One of Cheshire's curiosities, the 'Elephant and Castle' at Peckforton was carved in 1859 by John Watson, a stonemason working on Victorian Peckforton Castle. The stone for both came from the same local quarry. Over 12 feet (4 metres) high, the elephant with its odd fringed ears, is carved from a single block of stone, the castle on its back from three separate pieces.*

*When it was new, the hollow turreted castle had glass in every one of its windows. The impressive carving was intended to be used as a beehive; though there is no evidence that it ever was.*

*An elephant with a castle on its back featured in the coat of arms of the Corbett family, who were owners of Peckforton until about 1626.*

*Between the wars an attempt was made to buy the carving and ship it to America; happily the owners resisted the lure of dollars, and the elephant remained in its native Cheshire. Now a Grade II listed monument, the statue is due for conservation work.*

**SJ 538567** From the elephant follow the road for 50 metres towards Beeston Castle, and then turn L up Hill Lane. The tiny black and white house opposite was the old blacksmith's shop; today it's still called Smithy Cottage. Not far behind the smithy was Peckforton Mill, a water mill whose wheel was turned by the River Gowy.

Evidence of a far older people using the area was turned up in 1901, when a local farmer found a Neolithic stone-hammer in a cart load of clover from a nearby field. Finely polished, and 4.5 inches (11 cms) long, it had been made of Cumberland granite over 4,000 years ago.

Hill Lane winds uphill between steep banks clad in ferns and cow parsley; while overhanging damson trees in the autumn fill the road with purple windfallen fruit. A silence, broken only by the crowing of a distant cockerel, evokes a rural past when every lane in this part of

Cheshire was just as narrow. Local reminiscences tell of the horses of the hunt leaping clear over the lanes from bank to bank.

Until the 1830s there were at least four cottages on Hill Lane; only one is left - a house with spikey house-leeks covering part of its roof. A little further on, beyond a young conifer plantation on the L, is a small, hedged-in hollow on the R, the site of one of the vanished homes. Only tall docks and white-umbelled hogweeds mark the place today.

**SJ 533566**  Soon the track begins to climb more steeply. In summer the leaves of tall oaks and sycamores dapple the ground. As the road ascends, its surface deteriorates: old tree trunks are laid crossways, with huge stones, to slow the winter' streams. It's as if the lane, too, is slipping back in time. Tawny owls shelter in the trees above; come this way at dusk and you may hear them scuffling about in the branches overhead, or see a dark silhouette floating out over the fields to the L. Even during the day the path is sometimes crossed by the rank, sharp must of a hunting fox - a distinctive country smell.

To make the climb easier for horse-drawn carts, the track was surfaced with locally quarried sandstone. Look for the gutters down either side; and then see how, despite this, a century of rains has eroded meandering gulleys between the stones. Leaf-mould is slowly covering the edges of the track, reclaiming the ground for plants and nature.

**SJ 532566**  Towards the top two narrower tracks branch off to the R; they lead to secluded Waste Hill Farm, once known as the Pheasantry, where the head gamekeeper for the Peckforton Estates lived. The adjoining kennels have since vanished.

**SJ 531566**  Gnarled oaks and ancient birches fringe the narrowing track. On either side are walls of carefully squared sandstone blocks, green with mosses and algae, and streaked with grey lichen. At the top a solidly-built stone bridge crosses Hill Lane. Listen for the echo beneath. Known locally as the Haunted Bridge, the story goes that a ghostly servant woman walks from the ruins of a stone hut (still visible

~~~~~~~~~~~~~~~~~~~~~~~~~~~~~~~~~~~~~~~~~~~~~~~~~~~~~~

among the trees on the R past the bridge) along the sandy track and up the bank on the far side; under her arm she carries her own severed head. Local superstition says that if you see her you'll be dead within the year.

The bridge was built in the 1850s to take horse-drawn carriages from the newly built Peckforton Castle to the gatehouse at the Peckforton Gap. Nearby was a light railway-line which carried building-stone to the Castle from Firbank Quarry, deep in the woods on the L.

**SJ 528566** Past the bridge the track becomes sandy and levels out. Outcrops of the underlying sandstone, worn smooth by generations of cartwheels and feet, push up through the path. This sunny, open part of the track follows an ancient route over the Peckforton Hills (see the map). Leading directly from Alpraham, Bunbury, and Spurstow to Burwardsley, Tattenhall and then Chester, it was part of the 'Walesmansway' or 'Walchmonstreet' - Welshman's way, *"a route for the trade in salt between the Cheshire 'wiches' (salt towns) and Wales."* Local people, too, walked this way to Chester market - 28 miles (45 kms) there and back!

At dusk on a warm summer's evenings the lane is filled with tiny bats, Pipistrelles - Cheshire 'Bit bats', patrolling their figure-of-eight beats for insects. Listen carefully and you may hear their high-pitched echo-location calls.

**SJ 526566** Soon the path tilts imperceptibly downhill, past an estate-worker's house. Go through the gate-way that straddles the track. The lane is once more metalled, and slopes more steeply now. A tapestry of briars and foxgloves cloaks the sandstone walls to the R.

Go past two cottages: white-painted 'Elephant Track, Burwardsley' cottage, and prim 'Rock Cottage'. The lane, icy here in winter, cuts through the bedrock, 12 feet (3.5 metres) deep in places, and winds on downhill past a derelict farm. At the next junction the wide vista of the Cheshire Plain opens out ahead - a chessboard of green fields edged by trees - towards Wales and the Dee.

**SJ 523565** Continue on until another, muddled, junction of lanes by a house. Go R, downhill for 50 metres, and then R again. Ahead is the lovely, out-of-the-way Pheasant Inn at Burwardsley, a former black and white farmhouse with a block for mounting horses still outside. Not so long ago it was still known as the Carden Arms, after the old Cheshire Carden family. The pub is a good place from which to watch the sun set behind the distant Welsh mountains; and if it's raining, it's a good place anyway.

**SJ 523566** From the Pheasant Inn, once refreshed, retrace your steps until you come to the Haunted Bridge. At most times of the year there is enough light to see by even when the sun has gone down. But don't linger too long by the bridge.

**SJ 531566** Immediately past the bridge, a stile climbs into the adjacent fields; it's signposted 'Stonehouse Lane, Bulkeley'. An ancient lane called 'Baws Lane' originally ran from here, along the forest edge and on down to Stonehouse Farm, on the Bulkeley road. Several cottages stood along the lane; and it was in the garden of one of these cottages that the stone elephant once stood. It was moved to its present position in about 1890, when the cottages were demolished.

But, for us another footpath runs diagonally downhill across the pasture. Head for the two oaks just visible in mid-field, peeping over the brow of the hill. Little owls, introduced into this country in the 1890s, can sometimes be seen perched in their branches. The hill is popular, too, as a sledge run in winter, when the steep bluff at the bottom can prove treacherous. Follow the slope down towards the large clump of trees at the bottom.

**SJ 537565** Over a stile, look down into the now disused quarry where sandstone was cut for the local houses; it's at least 40 feet (12.5 metres) deep, but now full of scrub and brambles.

**SJ 538565** We are once more on 'Walesmansway', a route used by, among others, the famous itinerant preacher, John Wesley. He preached at Bunbury and the surrounding villages - said to be the birthplace of

~ ~ ~ ~ ~ ~ ~ ~ ~ ~ ~ ~ ~ ~ ~ ~ ~ ~ ~ ~ ~ ~ ~ ~ ~ ~ ~ ~ ~ ~ ~ ~ ~ ~ ~ ~ ~ ~ ~ ~ ~ ~ ~ ~ ~ ~

Primitive Methodism in Cheshire - in October 1749. Beyond another stile look for a massive oak tree on the L. A gnarled leviathan with a giant trunk, it is at least 16 feet (5 metres) in girth. John Wesley is said to have preached beneath its, even then, ancient branches. Once the old way over the hills, leading up via Peckforton Hall Lane from the ancient salt town of Nantwich and on into Wales, the route passed a number of churches on its way.

Two further stiles, one a curious stone and oak ladder, take us past Bank Cottages, with their ancient pear trees and neat potato patches, back into Peckforton village. Once back out on the road, turn L; your car is parked ahead. Look for the Victorian postbox built into the wall, with its telltale ornate VR on the front. It's another reminder of the history of Peckforton. But before you leave, think how pleasant it would be if the black and white cottage on the corner was still used for its original purpose: it used to be another pub, called the White Horse. Then we might have called this walk: "From the Stone Elephant to The Pheasant, and then all the way back to the White Horse".

*Spanning ancient 'Walesmonsway' as it ascends the Peckforton Hills is the Haunted Bridge - built in the 1850's to carry the carriage drive to Peckforton Castle.*

69

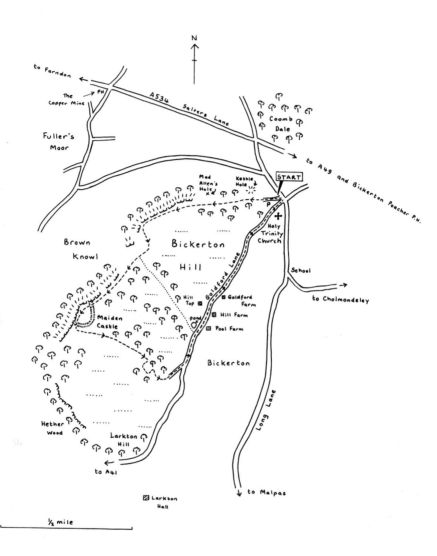

# Bickerton

# 7 Bickerton ~ *from Mad Allen's Hole to the Maiden's Castle* ~

Ice Age 'kettle hole', hermit's cave, Iron Age hillfort, views, breezes and bilberries.

> **Start:** *Bickerton, 4 miles (6 kilometres) north of Malpas. Map reference* **SJ 510536.**
> **Distance**: *2.5 miles (4 kilometres).*
> **Duration**: *2 hours.*
> **Maps:** *OS 1:50,000 Landranger Sheet 117 Chester; OS 1:25,000 SJ 55.*
> **Terrain:** *Long ascent to ridge, undulating hilltop, dry sandy paths; usually dry.*
> **Food and Drink:** *Bickerton Poacher, Wrexham Road, Bickerton. Map reference* **SJ 524545.** *Freehouse. Good food, bar snacks, restaurant. Children welcome. Tel: Cholmondeley 226.*

Bees hum over the heather on these high hills; an echo of a distant time when the local names Bickley and Bickerton meant 'Bee-keeper's Field' and 'Bee-keeper's Farm'. Generations later, in Norman times, the name was still *Bicretone* - a bee-sounding word. On a summer's afternoon, the drone of insects replaces the drum of cars and seems to carry the hills back in time. For a moment the clock is arrested and it could be any afternoon in history.

The Bickerton Hills are formed of overlying, tilted beds of sandstone: Keuper and Bunter Mottled Sandstones, Pebble Beds and Waterstones. Created at the bottom of a shallow sea some 225 million years ago in the Triassic period, and then tilted upwards, the rocks were later scoured by glaciers during successive Ice Ages. The softer rocks

~ ~ ~ ~ ~ ~ ~ ~ ~ ~ ~ ~ ~ ~ ~ ~ ~ ~ ~ ~ ~ ~ ~ ~ ~ ~ ~ ~ ~ ~ ~ ~ ~ ~ ~ ~ ~ ~ ~ ~ ~

became valleys; the harder rocks became hills.

When early man arrived, the Cheshire valleys were still covered with peat-mosses and marshland, formed by water collecting in the undrained glacial boulder clays. In contrast, the sandstone hills seemed a hospitable place: high and dry, with easily tilled soils, open mixed oak-woodland and springs of clear water, bubbling up from the aptly named Waterstones at their foot. All six of the early Iron Age hillforts recognised in Cheshire occupy high points along the ridge; in those days the hills were the place to be.

**SJ 510536** Our walk starts at the tiny village of Bickerton, stretched along the dip slope of the hills, 4 miles (6.5 kms) north of Malpas.

Turn off the A 534 Wrexham to Nantwich road as it crests the gap between the Bickerton and Bulkeley hills, not far from Gallantry Bank. Still known locally as Salters Lane, the A 534 used to be one of the old salt roads from Nantwich into Wales. Now, an old cast-iron sign points to 'Bickerton Church', 'Cholmondeley 4' and 'Malpas 4.5'.

At the bottom of the hill, cross the Broxton to Cholmondeley road into Goldford Lane, and park on a triangle of gravel just past Bickerton church. Until 1843, Bickerton was part of the huge parish of Malpas, with its 25 townships. Holy Trinity church, built in 1839, is a 'chapel of ease' - so called because it meant the villagers no longer had to travel long distances to church on a Sunday. The one acre cemetery was added later on, in 1880. Today the straggling village of Bickerton is still attractive; and three signs on a post by the churchyard wall boast: 'Best Kept Village 1977, 1981, 1982'.

**SJ 510536** Opposite the church a sign points uphill, beside beech-hedged 'Bickerton Croft' house, to 'Larkton Hill'. For the next mile (1.5 kms) we follow the Sandstone Trail with its symbol of a black footprint on a yellow ground. Over a stile the sandy path winds uphill through mixed oak and birch woodland. Orange-berried rowans startle the eye; while outcrops of sandstone and gnarled roots, worn smooth by walkers, push up through the thin soil.

**SJ 508535** A hundred metres on, the path snakes around a deep pit to the R. Called a 'kettle hole', it's a reminder of the last Ice Age. As the glaciers retreated a huge chunk of ice was left behind, half buried among the sand and rock; and when it melted this unusual basin remained.

The large shed in the field to the R is a helicopter hangar; look for the concrete apron in front, and the wind sock - to tell the pilot the pre-take-off wind direction - on the brow of the hill beyond.

**SJ 506536** As the path starts to climb more steeply, the feet of innumerable walkers have worn an 8 feet (2.5 metres) deep defile into the slope, showing how the old hollow ways were created. A rounded ledge of rock juts from the eroded path, and already people have started a detour to the L.

Soon the path levels, climbs, then levels out again. Jays scream among the trees. And then, on the R as we approach the top, hints of the impressive view beyond appear between the trunks - a flickering panorama like some Victorian picture-making toy.

**SJ 503535** The path dips alongside a 20 foot (6 metre) cliff. Over the years unthinking youths have carved their names and initials into the soft sandstone: PIG, ER, 'Dave + Sal 72' and naughty 'Deborah'. Down the briar and fern clad slope to the R is Mad Allen's Hole, a curious man-made, two level cave cut into the cliff. To reach it requires a wild scramble through the brambles, and is only for the hardy. Halfway down the slope, go around the cliff face to the R. The cave is hidden behind a huge moss-grown slab that has crashed down from the rock-face above, and is difficult to find.

**SJ 503536** Mad Allen's Hole is said to have been once occupied by a young man who lost his sanity when both sets of parents objected to his marriage to the girl he loved. He shunned society, sold all his belongings, and retired to a cave where he died 70 years later.

In fact he moved several times, from one cave to another, as a letter in an old Cheshire newspaper suggests:

> *"In or about the year 1809 ... strange stories were afoot as to a hermit who had been discovered in Allenscombe's Cave, in the parish of Harthill; that he had secreted himself there, as he had previously done in a similar cave near to Carden cliff. After remaining a self-made alien in his own country for so long, the whereabouts of his hermitage was accidentally discovered, and the sanctity of his rocky home was soon invaded by strangers."*

It would seem that, irritated by these invasions, he moved to the Bickerton cave - Mad Allen's Hole - only towards the end of his life.

Another source offers a more prosaic interpretation. It claims, "*... the name is taken from a man hired by a local landlord to impersonate a hermit in an artificial cave here.*" In fact, it's not such a far-fetched claim; for an 18th century fad for the picturesque meant rich patrons did sometimes fill their estates with hermits and grottoes. You must choose your favourite story.

**SJ 502535** On along the edge, the path opens onto heathland dotted with rowans and small oaks. Purple and mauve heather and ling contrast with the emerald bracken; and swallows and martins swirl above the lip of the scarp in summer. Except on the calmest of days, the breeze that beats in over the edge from the Welsh hills dominates the senses.

And the view ...! It's a delight. To the north the line of the hills stretches past Raw Head and Harthill to Kelsall, Delamere, Frodsham and Helsby. On the distant Mersey, look for the Fiddlers Ferry power-station cooling towers and further round, on the horizon, the vast tower of Liverpool's Anglican Cathedral. Around to the L the panorama takes in Chester and the Welsh hills - including Jubilee Tower-topped Moel Famou - and, in front, the broad farmlands of the valley of the Dee. Use the map to work out other landmarks.

~ ~ ~ ~ ~ ~ ~ ~ ~ ~ ~ ~ ~ ~ ~ ~ ~ ~ ~ ~ ~ ~ ~ ~ ~ ~ ~ ~ ~ ~ ~ ~ ~ ~ ~ ~ ~ ~ ~

Also below, close to the bottom of the hill, are a line of springs and wells that have supplied water since time immemorial. More recently (1946-54), deep boreholes have been sunk by the Staffordshire Potteries Water Board; small square brick buildings cover the boreholes, and can be seen between Bickerton and the Peckforton Pumping Station.

Aerial surveys made during the drought summer of 1976 showed an undefended Bronze Age settlement close to Rawhead, just to the north; and a possible Roman signalling station nearby. Both are further evidence of the attraction of this area to early man.

The path curves along the top of the hill, and then downhill out of the wind. Here, the delicate woody scent of the heather evokes the summer moorlands and mountains of a lifetime.

**SJ 501533** A hundred metres on, a four-fingered signpost points R, down a broad, well worn sandy track to 'Larkton Hill'. Shortly, it meets another, still broader track running up from Bickerton, and on over the hill, signposted to 'Brown Knoll' and the 'Copper Mine Inn'. We go straight over, uphill again, and on towards Maiden Castle.

**SJ 500531** When the path forks, go R, up a sharp slope, and out onto an undulating, still rising plateau. Earlier this century, these tops were grazed by sheep. But now each year this area seems to get more overgrown with birch scrub and bracken; and the bilberries are pushed back. It's perhaps the best place in Cheshire for these subtle-flavoured fruits. The low, dark green bushes are covered with purple berries (in fact, the expanded calyx of the flower) in early July. Some years are better than others. In the best years even the birds glut themselves; and their lurid purple droppings decorate the sandstone outcrops and paths with abstract splashes.

**SJ 499531** The path climbs steadily along the edge, then dips down to skirt a small indentation in the slope.

**SJ 497529** At the top of the next rise, 694 feet (216 metres) above

75

sea-level, is the Iron Age camp of 'Maiden Castle'. Heather and birch scrub hide the earthworks today, and many walkers are unaware of the existence of the fort .

> *"... whose turfed and cowslipped rampart seems,*
> *more hill than history, ageless and oblivion blurred."*

The last century has seen the ramparts further eroded; as late as 1819, the Cheshire historian Ormerod noted the *"... perfect state of the works."* Only in 1982 was the land given to the National Trust; now the hillfort should be safe.

*Excavation of Maiden Castle Iron Age hillfort at Bickerton in 1934-5 exposed the 2,500 years old inturned main entrance, with its massive drystone-walled revetment.* (Photograph courtesy of Canon M.H.Ridgway.)

~~~~~~~~~~~~~~~~~~~~~~~~~~~~~~~~~~~~~~~~~~~~~~~~~~~~~

# Maiden Castle ~ An Iron Age Hillfort

*Maiden Castle is a hillfort rather than a castle; and was a defended village of the Iron Age Cornovii tribe in the centuries before the Roman conquest.*

*Precipices defend the diminuitive 1.5 acres (0.6 hectares) hillfort to the north-west; whilst two curving ramparts, each with its own ditch, protect the shallow south-eastern slopes. Excavations by Liverpool University, in 1934-35 and again in 1962, showed the inner bank was originally 17 feet (5 metres) wide and 12 feet (4 metres) high, with some kind of palisade along the top. Massive drystone walling supported a bank of sand and boulders interlaced with deliberately charred branches. The outer rampart had a similar drystone wall at the front but not at the back.*

*The main entrance was an inturned sunken passage with a cobbled surface, that pierced both banks on the north-east side. It was defended by at least one pair of stout gates and a guard chamber. Further excavation in 1980 uncovered a small postern-gate entrance along the cliff edge at the other end of the camp.*

*Quarrying for stone inside the fort, sometime in recent history, has obliterated much of the original ground surface; but traces survive of large circular houses built probably of wattle and daub, with thatched rooves and south-east facing porches designed to catch the warmth of the early morning sun.*

*The people who lived in them were farmers and hunters, who perhaps traded in salt and pottery. Much like the Gaulish tribes in Julius Caesar's accounts, the men probably indulged in seasonal ritualised warfare, while the women did most of the work!*

And why is it called Maiden Castle? Various explanations have been offered. The correct one is that it's an old name, Maegden Castle, meaning a virgin or untaken fort. Local folklore makes the alternative suggestion that, in the absence of their men, the fort was once defended by the women alone. But best is the perhaps tongue-in-cheek explanation of a Victorian wag: *"Maiden Castle",* he wrote, *"offers a privacy where maidens may indulge their fancy"*. Racy stuff indeed for a staid Victorian! What could he have been thinking of?

Where the steep edge - quarried for building stone long after the Iron Age - peters out, we cross the defences again, and drop down to an open heath. Embedded in a boulder here, a National Trust plaque recaps the hillfort's history.

**SJ 497528**  The path splits off in three directions; we go L, away from the edge. This area was recleared only a few years ago, to form a semi-open heath. Already this has attracted the rare nightjar or 'goatsucker' - a nocturnal, moth-eating, migrant bird - back to these summer hills.

*Amid the honey-scented heather, two paths lead to the once formidable inturned entrance of Maiden Castle's Iron Age hillfort.*

Fifty metres on, the hillfort's still imposing double ramparts curve away into the bracken and heather, splashed with the vibrant yellow of gorse in flower. No horses are allowed on the fort, but hoof prints pattern the adjacent broad sandy track as it weaves downhill and into

~~~~~~~~~~~~~~~~~~~~~~~~~~~~~~~~~~~~~~~~~~~~~~

the birch woods.

**SJ 501527**  Under the trees, the track passes rough pasture to the R. A hefty trunk slung on chains blocks the passage of any wheeled vehicles that try to come this way. Soon afterwards, the track bends R, around the bottom of the field; and fifty metres later it meets a dog-leg in a gravelled lane.

**SJ 502526**  Three signs on a post here reassure us that 'Larkton Hill' also belongs to the National Trust. Go L, downhill. The lane sweeps L, then R, then L again, around the honeysuckle-entwined hedges of three large houses with small names like 'The Cottage'. And suddenly a new view appears: the Welsh hills around to the R  and, like an iceberg on the southern horizon, the vast bulk of the Wrekin, away in Shropshire.

**SJ 504525**  At the bottom of the slope the gravelled track comes out on Goldford Lane. Turn L past a loose group of tiny cottages almost lost in lush flower gardens.

**SJ 505527**  Two hundred metres on, the narrow lane reaches an open area opposite Pool Farm, where tall hornbeams overhang a farm pond on which white water-lilies grow. From here a sandy track, sign-posted to 'Bickerton Hill, Sandstone Trail', makes an attractive alternative route to Maiden Castle.

But we continue along Goldford Lane, past Hill Farm, Goldford Farm and Hill Top. And then past the converted, wartime Nissen hut of agricultural engineers, 'Ernest Proctor and Sons', where yellow and blue tractors are parked outside in haphazard abandon. Above them, to the L, rise the dense birch woods of the Bickerton Hills.

**SJ 510536**  Half-a-mile (1 km) later, and we are back at Bickerton church and the start of our walk. It's a charming part of Cheshire. So let's go round again, to Mad Allen's Hole, the hillfort, the bilberries and the view. It won't take long.

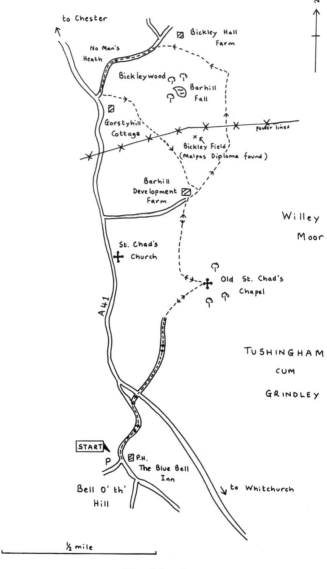

N

to Chester

No Man's Heath

☒ Bickley Hall Farm

Bickley wood

Barhill Fall

☒ Gorstyhill Cottage

power lines

Bickley Field (Malpas Diploma found)

Barhill Development Farm

Willey Moor

St. Chad's Church

A 41

Old St. Chad's Chapel

TUSHINGHAM
CUM
GRINDLEY

START

P

☒ P.H. The Blue Bell Inn

Bell O' th' Hill

to Whitchurch

½ mile

**Tushingham**

# 8 Tushingham ~ *dead ducks and diplomas* ~

Ancient inn, ghostly duck, cavalier's hat, lost roads, rare Roman diploma, bottomless pit and isolated chapel.

---

**Start:** *Bell o' th' Hill, 3 miles (5 kilometres) north of Whitchurch. Map reference* **SJ 523454.**

**Distance**: *3.5 miles (6 kilometres).*

**Duration**: *2 hours.*

**Maps:** *OS 1:50,000 Landranger Sheet 117 Chester; OS 1:25,000 Sheet SJ 54.*

**Terrain**: *Flat or gently undulating. Lanes and footpaths across pasture. Sandy and dry.*

**Food and Drink:** *The Blue Bell, Bell o' th' Hill, Tushingham. Map reference* **SJ 523455.** *Greenall Whitley. Hot and cold food. Tel: Whitchurch 2172.*

---

'Cheshire's Deep South' is the apt title of one of the County's tourist brochures which describes the area south of a line from Wrexham to Crewe. The clever phrase conjures up an image of hicks and hillbillies, corn bread and cat fish from the American south. But the Cheshire that abuts Clwyd and Shropshire is famous for other things: for its pastoral beauty, its black and white houses, its canals and its cheese. One of the finest dairy farming areas in Britain, south Cheshire has more cows to the acre than anywhere else in the world; or at least it did before EC milk quotas were introduced.

Friesian cows, the familiar and ubiquitous high-yielding black and white dairy cattle, are still common in the oak-punctuated pastures. Though most of the famous Cheshire cheese is today made in creameries, some local farms still produce the top quality 'Farmhouse' cheese.

Greener, quieter, and more fertile than north Cheshire, the south has an equally long, though perhaps less well documented, history. It seems steeped in the past; and even the Romans were here - as we shall discover.

**SJ 523454**  Our walk begins 18 miles (29 kms) south of Chester, and 3 miles (5 kms) north of Whitchurch, just inside the Cheshire border, at a tiny village called Bell o' th' Hill. Turn off the Chester to Whitchurch road - the A 41, just past the tall Victorian church at Tushingham. A new stretch of fast road by-passes the old village; and the loops of the old A41 seem unnaturally quiet. It's as if the new road has by-passed time, too, and carried a small island of Cheshire back into its rural past.

Park close to the Blue Bell Inn, a large half-timbered building on a bend in the road. It is one of the oldest inns in Cheshire. Ogilby's Britannia Roadbook, published in 1675, when this was the main highway from Chester to Whitchurch, Shrewsbury, Ludlow and Bristol, calls it *"Ye signe of Ye Bel"*. There are few houses here; and, according to the Women's Institute of the time, until the 1950s this tiny hamlet had, *"no mains water, no sewerage, no electricity, no telephone kiosk, no Post Office, no surgery and no new houses"*.

Inside, the ancient Blue Bell Inn is as yet unspoilt. Low doorways connect a maze of rooms, and the main bar still features an inglenook fireplace. On the walls are old photographs and a miscellany of outmoded farm implements: rick cutters, pail yokes and dung forks; while in a case are a leather Cavalier's hat, and a 400 years old mummified rat that was found curled in a wall cavity.

Stranger still is the tale of the resident ghost, not of a human but of a duck! A fluffy duckling was brought up in a basket by the fire, but as it grew so it became more territorial. It pecked at people's ankles until eventually it was killed and buried at the bottom of the cellar stairs. But neither the step nor the duck would "stay put". And having escaped, the ghostly duck would run about making a nuisance of itself in the old way, pecking spectrally at people's ankles. So twelve parsons were

~~~~~~~~~~~~~~~~~~~~~~~~~~~~~~~~~~~~~~~~~~~~~~~~~~~~~

called in to "pray it down". Each held a lighted candle, and as they prayed the duck got smaller and smaller, until it could be popped into a bottle. The bottle was tightly corked and bricked up in a wall. And, by all accounts, it's still there today, with the duck's ghost inside. Whisky is not the only spirit in this pub.

**SJ 523457** From the 'Blue Bell', turn R and follow the curves of the now mud-bespattered and almost deserted old A41. Three hundred metres later, turn R up a narrow lane signposted 'Sandstone Trail'. Within 50 metres it meets the new by-pass; cross carefully, it's a busy road.

**SJ 524458** Beyond the new A41 the lane continues out into the fields, and the roar of traffic soon fades away. Eight species of native tree or bush can be found in the hedges on either side here; and, in places, even though the ground is level, the lane is 2 feet (60 cms) below field level. Bluebells and dogs mercury grow under the hedge - both are so-called 'ancient woodland indicators'. All of which suggest the lane's antiquity.

**SJ 525461** At the lane's end, 400 metres later, go through the wooden kissing gate signed with a yellow arrow - a subsidiary footpath marker. The lane didn't always end here; when the old Tithe Map was surveyed in 1838 the lane continued via Barhill Farm to Gorstyhill Cottages - the latter stretch of which is still a bridleway today.

Beyond the gate, rolling countryside, latticed with hedges and tall ashes and oaks, spreads away to the south and east. This undulating pasture is brown hare country; with their jacked-up back legs and black-tipped ears, they are easily distinguished from the rabbits. While, in summer, swallows flit in low arcs across the grass, hawking for flies.

At the end of the last Ice Age the lower ground to the east was covered by a meltwater lake; remnants today are picturesque Bar-, Marbury- and Quiosley Meres.

**SJ 527463** Nestled among trees on the far side of the field is lonely

St. Chad's chapel. Enter the churchyard through the white-painted wicket gate. The garage-like building on the L was originally a meeting house; it now protects the old horse-drawn parish hearse - once known locally as the 'Black Maria'. Church owls - better known today as barn owls - used to nest in the secluded belfry; sadly they no longer do. But perhaps the old superstition is still held locally, that to see one close to the village was an omen of an impending death.

# Old St. Chad's, Tushingham

*Tushingham was part of the ancient parish of Malpas, one of the largest medieval parishes in the County. Because it was so large, chapels of ease like St. Chad's were built to save people an over-long Sunday walk.*

*During the nineteenth century the medieval parishes were subdivided. A new Victorian church, again dedicated to St. Chad, was built on the main road in 1860-63, leaving the old chapel stranded in the fields. The new church has no graveyard, and old St. Chad's remains the parish burial ground. The shape and character of the burial ground suggest it may be of Saxon origin.*

*A far older timber-framed church originally stood on the site; it may have been a chantry chapel, as fields nearby are still called the Chantry Fields. In 1689 it was rebuilt in brick using money given by a local man who had made good in London. The stairs outside lead to an internal gallery which, along with two private box-pews, was used by local gentry. All the furniture is original 17th century.*

*With no heating or lighting, monthly services are held here only during the summer. The most popular is Rushbearing Day in August - an ancient ceremony, when freshly-cut rushes are strewn on the floor.*

*Stranded in the middle of fields at Tushingham, Old St. Chad's chapel was once home to nesting barn owls.*

Old St. Chad's inaccessibility is unusual. But Ogilby's 1675 route map shows that the old road from Whitchurch to Chester once ran further to the east than the C18th turnpike (or toll road) that replaced it, and which is now the modern A41. The old road has long since been ploughed up. Yet the locality is riddled with pathways, some of which are based on Roman civil roads and tracks. After the Romans left, horses, cattle and carts kept them in daily use for centuries.

The sloping field behind the chapel is called Hollywell Ridding, and there's a pond at the bottom; perhaps the name hints at early Celtic water worship at a holy well or spring.

**SJ 526464**  Leaving the ancient churchyard, strike out diagonally to the R, across the field. Head for the stile and signpost visible halfway along the distant hedge. Once at the stile, the signpost points back towards 'Grindley Brook'  and L to the 'A41, Main Road'. We continue towards 'Bickley Wood'.

**SJ 526468**  Two stiles later, the path emerges on a farm lane by the tall, white farmhouse at Barhill Developmental Farm, where they test cattle feeds. Farmworkers tell how 'Animal Liberationists' have raided the farm, misunderstanding the innocuous nature of their work. Follow the Sandstone Trail on downhill between the sheds.

Emerging from the farmyard, the track curves northwards. Don't touch the electric fences along its edges; especially in wet weather they can give you an unpleasant shock. At the bottom another stile, next to the middle of the three gates, takes the path on uphill, and we cross the Tushingham cum Grindley parish boundary.

**SJ 527472**  Tall thistles and poisonous foxgloves (from which a heart drug is made) splash the hedge with purple. Here the path goes under an unsightly power line that marches off to the west. Beside the first pylon in the field to the L - called Bickley Field - is a dip. It was just here, according to a local farmhand, that the so-called Malpas Diploma was found in 1812.

86

*Now preserved in the British Museum in London, the Malpas Diploma was found close to the Barhill Downfall at Tushingham in 1812. It grants citizenship to a Roman decurian, Reburrus the Spaniard, for 25 years' army service. (Reproduced by Courtesy of the Trustees of the British Museum).*

The bronze diploma, or military discharge certificate, is now preserved in the British Museum, in London; though a copy can be seen in Nantwich Museum. Such certificates were issued to auxiliary soldiers of the Roman army on completion of 25 years service and granted them and their descendants citizenship and legalized their marriages. Like other diplomas from Britain and abroad, they can tell

87

us where different army units were stationed at different periods. The Malpas Diploma was issued to a man called Reburrus, a junior cavalry officer - or decurio, of the First Pannonian Regiment from Spain, on the 19th of January, AD 103. The two bronze plates, each about 9 by 6 inches (23 by 15 cms), are hinged together by bronze rings. There is no evidence so far of a settlement in the area, and it seems likely the diploma was lost as Reburrus travelled north on the road from *Mediolanum*, or Whitchurch, in Shropshire, 2 miles (3 kms) away.

**SJ 527474** Under a big oak at the top of the field, go L over a stile. Thirty metres on, the path continues through a gate and rises diagonally to the R over rough pasture.

**SJ 525475** Look back to your L. Among a group of trees here is Barhill Fall - a reputedly bottomless pit. A contemporary account tells how, back in 1687, a farmer travelling slowly along the old cart road to church at St. Chad's Chapel was terrified by a *"huge noise"* behind him. Turning round, he saw that a small hillock had disappeared into the earth, leaving a yawning hole. The culprit was an underground stream that had eaten away at a vast saltbed, causing the land above to cave in. But imagine the farmer's ignorant terror; as hell gaped he must have feared that demons would swirl up out of the pit, and that his end had come.

White marker posts lead on to another stile in the dog-legged corner of a field. From here go L and follow the Sandstone Trail signs keeping to the L of the large Victorian farm. In summer scores of twittering house martins twist about the red brick barns; and sheep stare vacantly from the shade.

**SJ 523480** Past the farm the footpath opens onto a narrow road. But while the Sandstone Trail goes off to the R, we follow the signpost L towards 'Grindley Brook'.

**SJ 521472** A third of a mile (0.5 km) on, past Manor Farm, turn L just before the junction with the A41 at Gorstyhill Cottage. This little-used lane is a bridleway signposted as 'Willey Moor Lane'. It was originally a continuation of the sunken lane that leads from Bell o' th' Hill towards St Chad's chapel. Go through two gates, past a small farm and an orchard, and with the hedge on your L, pass once more back under the power lines. Beyond more stiles, head for white-painted Barhill Farmhouse, now with the hedges on your R. Rejoin the Sandstone Trail immediately below Barhill Farm; and watch out again for those electric fences!

**SJ 526468** Return through the farmyard and, turning off to the L, retrace your steps via the field containing old St. Chad's Chapel, to the Blue Bell Inn at Bell o' th' Hill. Perhaps, if you're lucky, it may still be open.

*The Blue Bell Inn at Bell o' th' Hill, one of Cheshire's oldest pubs, is mentioned in Ogilby's 1675 'Britannia Roadbook' as "Ye signe of Ye Bel".*

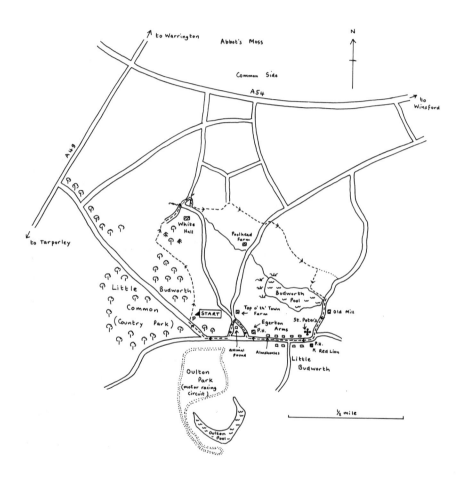

# Little Budworth

# 9 Little Budworth ~ *the remains of Mondrem* ~

Ancient common, sunken paths, mill pool, Romanies' meeting place, and the grave of the 'King of the Gypsies'.

**Start:** *Little Budworth, 2 miles (3 kilometres) west of Winsford. Near Oulton Park. Map reference SJ 592654.*
**Distance**: *3 miles (5 kilometres).*
**Duration:** *2 hours.*
**Maps:** *OS 1:50,000 Landranger Sheet 117 Chester; OS 1:25,000 SJ 56.*
**Terrain:** *Mostly flat; woodland paths, sandy tracks, field paths, quiet roadside. Usually dry, but muddy in winter.*
**Food and Drink:** *Red Lion Hotel, Little Budworth. Map reference SJ 599654. Homemade food at lunch and evenings (except Sundays). Tel: 0289 760275. Or The Egerton Arms, Little Budworth. Free house. Beer garden, meals; open evenings on weekdays only. Tel: 0289 760250.*

Four forests covered much of Cheshire in the time of the Norman Domesday Book. Wirral Forest to the west had been mainly cleared. Otherwise, apart from the as yet still sparsely inhabited Dee and Weaver valleys, most of the county was wild and wooded. Primeval Macclesfield Forest clothed the Pennines' eastern slopes. While a large part of central Cheshire, between the Mersey on the north and the Gowy and Weaver rivers to the west and east, formed the two forests of Mara (now Delamere) and Mondrem.

But they weren't forests in the way we think of them today; there were no dark ranks of Forestry Commission conifers, and even the original mixed oak woodlands were patchy, with large areas of open heath dotted with boggy pools and meres. 'Forest' was no more than a legal term; and forests were simply waste-lands ruled over by harsh laws that protected them for the hunting of a privileged few.

Nor were the ancient forests as tame and homogenised as modern Delamere. Wolf packs hunted among the trees as late as the 14th century. Both red and fallow deer browsed Mara and Mondrem until they were hunted out in the 17th century, during the Civil War. And among the recorded perks of a forester granted land at Little Budworth in 1153, were the rights to: "*all sparrowhawks, merlins, hobbys, and swarms of bees*". Rare birds indeed.

Little Budworth was part of Mondrem. Until the 1800s it was called Budworth-le-Frith - from a Welsh word *ffridd,* meaning something like 'upland common brought under cultivation'; and in 1650, nearby Oulton was also known as Ferneleghes, or the 'ferny clearings'. Forest clearance and settlement continued throughout the Middle Ages until, by the 17th century, Mondrem was no longer forest. Only one last vestige remained, unclaimed, unfarmed, and unbuilt upon; the poorest and most worthless part, a wasteland: Little Budworth Common. It was the last remains of Mondrem.

Our walk begins outside the charming village of Little Budworth, close to Oulton Park motor-racing circuit, and just off the A 49 Warrington to Whitchurch road. Follow the signs for Oulton Park. A car park at the southern end of the old Coach Road that cuts across Little Budworth Common, near the imposing white-painted Georgian gatehouse to Oulton Park, provides toilets and an information board. A sign on a bank announces: 'Little Budworth Country Park'. Park here.

**SJ 591654** From the car park, go through a narrow gap in a fence, marked with a black footprint and arrow on a yellow background. A notice informs us: "*This Country park is a Site of Special Scientific Interest. Under the Wildlife and Countryside Act it is an offence to take, damage or injure any plant, tree, animal, or bird in any way or to deposit litter or rubbish of any sort*". Birches, gangling oaks, ferns and the whippy canes of wild raspberries rim the winding path. This is poor soil, almost pure sand - a legacy of the last Ice Age - overlain by a thin layer of leaf mould; and the barley fields beyond the trees to the R must rely entirely on artificial fertilisers to grow at all.

**SJ 589658** The path snakes past a padlocked gate. Soon afterwards, an area of cleared birch scrub, on the L, has been reclaimed by purple, honey-scented heather and ling, interspersed with splashes of yellow gorse. Harebells and yellow-petalled tormentil grow in the open patches; with foxgloves, honeysuckle and wood sage under the damper edges. The woods are good for fungi in the autumn. And, apart from wrens, chaffinches and tits, less common birds favour this unusual habitat - like woodcock, redpolls and tree pipits. Little Budworth Common is one of the best examples of lowland heath left in Cheshire; and larger, more typical open sandy areas can be seen on the other side of the Coach Road.

A hundred metres on, the path crosses a wider, metalled track. Through stately wrought-iron gates a short distance off to the R, an avenue of tall limes dignifies black-and-white White Hall. It's the former home of the Earls of Shrewsbury who, along with the Egertons of Oulton Park, were local landowners.

**SJ 587660** Go straight on, over the wider track. A hundred metres later, at a muddy junction with a second path, go R. The fragrant scent of honeysuckle fills the still air. Look for traces of the old cobbles along the side of the track. A little farther on, a signpost points off to the L towards the 'Coach Road', next to a clump of woodland edge hazel bushes.

We curve R, on down the track. Another hundred metres on, on the L, is old-fashioned, cream painted Gardener's Cottage. The stable yards behind belong to White Hall Livery Stables, where for the last 40 years or so polo ponies from the Cheshire Polo Club have been looked after between games. At 15 to 16 hands high, these beautiful horses are hardly ponies; the diminuitive name is one of affection. Watch them grazing peacefully in the surrounding fields and you'll realise why.

**SJ 589661** Continue on down a narrow path that dips between deep banks overhung with sycamores. There are ferns along the banks and birdsong in the hedgerows. This is a Cheshire from before the First World War; a countryside of horses and narrow, unsurfaced lanes. And when an ivy-clad cottage looms between dense hedges on the bank above, the image seems confirmed.

Soon we cross a hollow where watercress grows in profusion in a boggy stream; it was once exported as far as London, but don't eat it now for fear of liver fluke. We shall meet the same stream later, on its downhill course to Budworth Pool.

**SJ 589662** Beyond the hollow is another sunken junction. A track curves off to the L, but we go straight on, uphill. The track curves to the R, climbing beneath tall banks topped by rampant hawthorn 20 feet (6 metres) above us. Crab apples and blackberries - the makings of a pie, are tangled in the hedge.

All these paths are very old. The network of tracks and paths, both here and across the Common, are a reminder of the ancient open field and strip system, whereby land was shared out evenly. But by the 19th century leasehold and freehold tenure had mostly overtaken the old medieval system. Fewer men were farming, now as tenants; and though the largest farms in Little Budworth were still only 109 and 199 acres, the size of farms was steadily growing. The 1839 Tithe map completes the picture of a small group of prosperous tenants and owner occupiers. The countryside was changing; and the ordinary people of Little Budworth were getting poorer.

**SJ 590663** At the top of the slope the track runs on. But we go sharply to the R, back downhill, around a dog-leg overgrown with wild broom, and into an even deeper, narrower sunken path. Don't miss this important turning.

Blackberry shoots reach out over the oak and hazel-lined path. And, worn down by feet and hooves over the centuries, this sloping runnel of a path seems like a green crevice in the sandy soil.

~~~~~~~~~~~~~~~~~~~~~~~~~~~~~~~~~~~~~~~~~~~~~~~~~~~

**SJ 590662**  At the bottom the path opens out above a stream. Before it curves to the L, along a muddy stretch, climb over a stile signposted to 'Park Road'. Tall yellow buttercups, birds-foot trefoil and water-loving horsetails are rank in this boggy paddock.

Over a second stile, keep the field edge to the R, and climb the slope with the stream below. In the far corner of the field, cross another stile and follow the yellow arrow along the hedge.

*Little Budworth Common - now a country park - is an ancient relic of the great forests of Mara and Mondrem that covered central Cheshire in the Middle Ages.*

~~~~~~~~~~~~~~~~~~~~~~~~~~~~~~~~~~~~~~~~~~~~~~~~~~~~~~

**SJ 593663** A further stile to the R opens out onto a large field. Early maps show these modern fields to be the amalgam of several older pastures which, back in the 1800s, were unsuitable for anything except grazing. Head straight across the field for the gate to the L of Poolhead Farm. (As the name suggests, Budworth Pool was once larger than it is today).

**SJ 596661** At the gate, turn L along the road. A sign points back to 'White Hall Lane'. Keep to the wide grass verge, and then, 50 metres later, turn R, down a broad green lane. This was part of the old cattle drovers' road between Oswestry and Helsby. In the 18th century nearby 'Beggar's Bank' was a famous rendezvous for travelling people. The abundance in the area of such green lanes made Little Budworth Common a favourite *atchin-tans* or stopping place for the 'dukes of little Egypt', where they could park their *vardos* or covered wagons, and relax among their own people. For, until 1784, when the law was changed, it was a criminal offence merely to be a gypsy, and in earlier days many were executed. Imagine the tang of wood-smoke from their camp fires, the grazing ponies, and washing drying on the bushes.

**SJ 598658** The green lane runs on beneath tall ashes, then drops downhill to Budworth Pool. The high banks here are good for blackberries in September. When the path levels out, 1/4 mile (0.5 km) later, climb over a stile to the R, signposted for 'Budworth Mere'. Across a horse paddock, turn L, along the reed-fringed lake shore.

From medieval times Budworth Pool was important for its fish; but today Tarporley Angling Club fish for sport, not food. In around 1300, it was called *Walkemulnepoul* meaning 'watermill pool'. Beyond a stile, beneath tall willows on the opposite side of the road is what was, until the turn of the century, the old flour mill, now converted into an attractive home.

**SJ 599656** Turn R, up Mill Lane. At the top of the hill go R again, around the bend, and into Little Budworth. Until quite recently, only a few thatched cottages clung to the skirts of the church, perched on its rock outcrop above the mere. In 1841 there were only 74 houses and

~~~~~~~~~~~~~~~~~~~~~~~~~~~~~~~~~~~~~~~~~~~~~~~~~~~~~

330 people in the parish; two tailors, a shoemaker and a blacksmith. Opposite the Red Lion, which dates back to the 1700s, is the church of St. Peter, reached by a fine set of stone steps.

# Saint Peter's Church, Little Budworth

*Saint Peter's church belonged originally to the nunnery of St Mary's in Chester. The oldest part is the simple stone tower in Perpendicular style, with its carved faces and gargoyles. Built sometime between 1490 and 1526, it dates from the late Middle Ages. Until early this century there was an iron brazier mounted on the roof, which held a beacon for signalling in times of war.*

*In 1757 the church was described as* "a neat building of red stone, having a tower at the west end, with two side aisles supported by wooden pillars". *The body of the church was rebuilt in stone in 1800 in Georgian style, using huge blocks of stone 6 feet (2 metres) long; and was paid for by the wealthy merchant son of a local farmer.*

*Inside the church, which can be viewed by fetching the key from the post office, are a Georgian pulpit and a fine 17th century fluted font, carved from fossil marble. The rest of the old fittings were lost in the 1870 'restoration'.*

*More interesting, perhaps, is an account of 1757 that tells us,* "The churchyard of Little Budworth in Cheshire contains the grave of one who in his day and generation was 'King of the Gypsies'. This person, Henry Lovett, died in 1745 at the age of 85." *He died a Protestant and is buried, so an even older account tells us,* "On the north side of the Church Yard, by the Rails of it, opposite the Chancel, where lies a large Stone upon the Ground."

*The 16th century tower of St. Peter's church, Little Budworth, reflected in the reed-fringed mere.*

From the church, continue through the village, past the white-painted 'Old Vicarage' until, half a mile (1 km) later you come to the almshouses on the corner of Pinfold Lane. Built in 1740, they gave a home to 6 poor men and 6 poor women of the parish, with free medicine and coal, and an extra half a crown at Christmas.

98

~~~~~~~~~~~~~~~~~~~~~~~~~~~~~~~~~~~~~~~~~~~~~~~~~~~~~~~~~~~~~

**SJ 593654** Go R at the war memorial to the fallen of the "Great War of 1914-19", down Pinfold Lane. Close by is the attractive Egerton Arms, a free house, next door to 'Oulton Park Cricket Club'.

**SJ 593655** At the junction of Pinfold and Park Lanes, is the old pinfold. A plaque on the wall inside tells us that it is, *"an enclosure in which stray animals were impounded until claimed on the payment of a fine, which has existed on this site since the 17th century. Restored and repaired 1986."* Which brings to mind the story from elsewhere in Cheshire, of the squatter who, building a roof and chimney on a pinfold between sunset and sunrise, was able to claim it as his home.

From the pinfold go L, and then R, away from the village, towards Oulton Park. Over the hedge to the R is the village football field; with its two white goal posts, it slopes alarmingly into the wheat field beyond.

**SJ 590654** A hundred metres later are the beech-tree shaded ornamental gates to Oulton Park, designed by Vanburgh. Now a famous motor-racing circuit, Oulton Park was the former stately home of the Egertons, a prominent Cheshire family. Oulton Hall burned down twice, in 1720 and 1926, and the ruins were bombed in 1940, during the Second World War. The park, laid out by William Eames, a famous landscape gardener of his day, once contained a herd of 300 deer. It was taken over by the army during the Second World War, when it became the headquarters of the American general, Patton.

Opposite the gates, turn R, up the old Coach Road which was built in about 1740 as a drive to Oulton Hall. A hundred metres later turn back into the car park.

We've come full circuit: from motor cars to foot, horseback, cart and gypsy wagons, and back to motor cars again.

N

to Chester

to Manchester

Vale Royal Drive

Vale Royal
Locks

to Northwich

Rookery
Pool

old river

River Weaver Navigation

Site of
Abbey
Nun's grave

Vale Royal
House

Monk's
Well

START

St. Mary's
Church

Vale Royal Drive

Sand pit

Abbot's
Walk

Whitegate

to Plough Inn

to Winsford

½ mile

**Whitegate**

# 10 Whitegate ~ *where Vale Royal Abbey stood* ~

**Picturesque village, Nun's Grave and ghost, site of Vale Royal Abbey, wooded Weaver Valley, and prophecies of Nixon - the Cheshire seer.**

---

**Start:** *Whitegate, 5 miles (8 kilometres) south-west of Northwich. Map reference SJ 629694.*
**Distance:** *3 miles (5 kilometres).*
**Duration:** *3 hours.*
**Maps:** *OS 1:50,000 118 Stoke-on-Trent & Macclesfield area; OS 1:25,000 SJ 67 and 66.*
**Terrain:** *Mostly flat; drive, wooded farmland, sandy paths and riverbank. Muddy in places.*
**Food and Drink:** *The Plough Inn, Beauty Bank, Whitegate. Map reference SJ 624682. Greenall Whitley. Bar snacks and food. Tel: Sandiway 889455.*

---

A king's vow to the Virgin Mary marked the start of the as yet unfinished story of Vale Royal. As a young prince returning from crusade in the Holy Land, during the winter of 1263-4, King Edward I was caught in a violent storm in the Bay of Biscay. "Hear me, oh Blessed Virgin," he promised, "and, in humble gratitude, I shall build a convent for a hundred monks of the order of Cistercians." It seems his prayers were answered. For, as he struggled ashore, the last to land, he looked back in time to see his ship vanish beneath the crashing surf. Only two men survived. It was an experience strong enough to bind any prince of Christendom to his vow.

But the implementation of his promise was delayed. For no sooner had he escaped with his life than the Barons' Wars began, and both King

Henry and the Prince were held prisoner by Simon de Montfort. Only when he became King, five years later, was Edward (who was known as 'longshanks' because of his unusual height) able to found his new abbey. As Royal Earl of Cheshire, he chose initially a site at Darnhall in Delamere Forest. Later it was moved to Whitegate, above the River Weaver. Edward I called it the Vale Royal, and decreed, *"there shall be no monastery more royal than this one, in liberties, wealth and honour, throughout the whole world."*

Our walk begins at the picturesque village of Whitegate, between Northwich and Winsford - so named after the white gates that once led up to the abbey. Clustered around the village green are the church, school and two thatched black-and-white cottages, one of which dates from 1656. They nestle in a hollow among pools and tall trees, to form a perfect scene.

**SJ 629694** Park opposite St Mary's church. A medieval wooden church built on this site in the 14th century by the monks of Vale Royal Abbey was rebuilt twice, in 1728 and again in 1874. Today, a half-timbered porch leads to a heavily studded door dating back to the 18th century; while inside there is a splendid hammer-beam roof supported by eight original medieval pillars. Outside, a squat, shingled spire looks down through wrought-iron gates to the village green, the scene of today's Whitsun Fair maypole dances.

Across the green is stately Whitegate House, a 17th century building that was once an inn called The Rifleman. A rent book for 1853 records that the licensee was paid for 30 dinners at 1s 6d (7.5p), 24 quarts of ale at 8d (3p), and 43 pints at 4d (1.5p) - a lot of money in those days! Even so, the pub lost its licence in 1870 because Lady Delamere, the wife of the owner of Vale Royal House, objected to *"the unseemly behaviour of customers on the green."*

From the village walk up Vale Royal drive, past the converted sandstone gatehouse at its entrance. Flanked by an avenue of tall beeches and limes, the drive leads gently uphill past residential houses on Sutton Field road, and on towards Vale Royal House. The sun dapples

~~~~~~~~~~~~~~~~~~~~~~~~~~~~~~~~~~~~~~~~~~~~~~~~~

through the leaves, and pigeons 'coo' among the trees above.

**SJ 633695** A quarter of a mile (0.5 km) later, soon after the drive levels out, turn R over a stile. It's signposted 'public footpath' and is marked with a yellow arrow - others of which we follow for much of the walk. Head straight across the field, towards the woods. In late summer, fat-hen, knotgrass, wild charlock, pineapple-scented mayweed and heartsease pansies - all weeds of cultivated soil - strew the path's edge.

**SJ 634693** Two hundred metres later, turn L, along the edge of the trees. A painted sign, on one of the power-line posts to the R, reads, 'Please keep your dogs on leads'. Brambles and purple rose-bay willowherb decorate the margin of the wood.

Another 300 metres on, the woodland edge kinks to the R around a disused and overgrown sandpit. It was still in use in 1911, at a time when these fields were parkland. Somewhere under the surrounding fields, too, is the Whitegate Aviation Beacon, which guides planes in and out of Manchester Airport, on a bearing of 240 degrees.

**SJ 637694** Bear R, around the old sandpit, and head for the corner of the wood. Here, beneath tall oaks and hawthorns, climb over a stile into the trees and turn L. The floor of this mixed deciduous wood is open and sunny, and sweet with the scent of swathes of bluebells in early summer. Hidden among the lush growth are the large purple-mauve flowers of cranesbill. Follow the path along the woodland edge as it meanders between the trunks and over fallen trees. There are foxes, squirrels and badgers in these woods; though you will have to be sharp eyed to see them.

**SJ 638695** At the end of this narrow strip of trees, climb over another stile and go R, along the outside of the wood. For the next 250 metres our path follows the old Abbot's Walk, marked on early maps. Behind us and to the L, large, attractive houses are hidden among the trees, and the clock tower of Vale Royal House is just visible, peeping above the tall hedges.

**SJ 640694** Continue along the field edge, and notice the rich, dark soil of this aptly named Vale Royal. At a further stile follow the yellow arrow to the L, along another field boundary. Beyond a paddock where graceful grey horses graze, is another belt of darker trees. Tall scots pines mix with sessile oaks and sinister yews: this is part of the now overgrown ornamental gardens of Vale Royal House, and the site of the Victorian pheasantry and the far older Monks' Well.

Over the stile the footpath goes straight ahead, over the brow of the hill and down towards the River Weaver. Four oaks, each past their best, mark the line of the old hedgerow between what was once two fields.

**SJ 643698** At the bottom of the field, 300 metres on, the path enters the woods that half encircle the sloping field. Beyond a stile, the path runs obliquely into the trees to the L. It's well used and easier to follow now. To the R of the path, the wetter ground that slopes down to a loop of the old, uncanalised river, is clad in hazel, elder and rowan. Soon the path drops diagonally down a slope between dark rhododendrons. Glimpses of the placid water below show fishermen lining the banks in season, waiting patiently to catch big carp, bream and tench.

It's a peaceful spot, but the overhanging trees mean there are no anglers on this side. The path crosses a silted up brook full of black leaf-mould; water dribbles over a curved, brick-built weir into the river. Its ceaseless trickle echoes under the dank trees.

**SJ 641700** A minute later, and the path is once more on drier ground. Across the fields to the L, where less than ten years ago wild daffodils grew, the Gothic rooves and chimneys of Vale Royal House loom above the lip of the slope.

# Vale Royal Abbey and House

In its prime Vale Royal was the largest and wealthiest Cistercian Abbey in England. The foundation stone for the high altar was laid by Edward I in 1277 at a ceremony attended by barons, bishops and all the trappings of Plantagenet power. At the feast afterwards they ate roast porpoises.

Endowments of land between Winsford and Frodsham were made to support the Abbey; and over £38,000 in the money of the time - a vast sum - was spent on its construction over the next 50 years. But Edward's incessant wars drained the coffers, and by 1336, in the reign of his grandson, the walls of the church were still unroofed.

For a while the Black Prince breathed new life into the project, but in October 1360 a storm blew down the entire nave, and at the Prince's death in 1376, royal patronage ended. If it had been finished the church would have been both bigger and longer than Fountains Abbey, in Yorkshire.

After Henry VIII's dissolution of the monasteries in 1539, the monks were turned out and the property and land sold to Sir John Holcroft of Lancashire. Much of the Abbey was demolished; but substantial parts of the monks' quarters were incorporated into later buildings, and still exist, particularly in the cellars.

Two generations later the Cholmondeleys, a Cheshire family, bought Vale Royal; and here they entertained King James I in 1617 on his celebrated visit to the Cheshire salt mines. But soon afterwards, during the Civil War, Parliamentary forces sacked the house and burnt down part of one wing.

Archaeological excavations in 1911-12 and 1958 established the plan of the church laid out in 1278. Basically crucifrom, it had a central tower and two smaller towers above the west end, with cloisters on the south side of the nave. The site of the Nun's Grave - from which a ghost allegedly still walks today - marks the east end where the high altar once stood.

Nixon, the Cheshire prophet, is said to have been born in Whitegate in 1467. A mentally subnormal ploughboy, he is credited with some extraordinary prophesies which were made when he fell into a trance. Among them, he foretold that Vale Royal Abbey would become a ravens' nest; and it is true that in 1538 the estate was bought by the Holcrofts - whose crest was a raven!

*Looming over Vale Royal House is the Nun's Grave, one of the few remains of what was once the greatest Cistercian Abbey in all England.*

~~~~~~~~~~~~~~~~~~~~~~~~~~~~~~~~~~~~~~~~~~~~~~~~~~~~~~

Huge oaks twist their roots into the bank alongside the path as it undulates beside the old river. Over a stile the path winds down to the water's edge, out in the open again, where thickets of head-high rosebay willowherb stretch away on either side. Kingfishers nest nearby and the river margin is lush with yellow flag and watercress.

**SJ 639703** Four hundred metres later, when the path emerges at a stile, go R, out onto Vale Royal drive - which, though private, is also a public right of way in parts. To the L the drive leads back to Vale Royal House. Tall horsetails, descendants of the primitive plants that formed the coal beds in prehistoric times, rim the drive beneath smooth-trunked beeches and tangled rhododendrons. At dusk mists rise from the river to drift over the path.

**SJ 639706** Cut down to the river, 500 metres later - to the R, and cross the old arm of the Weaver by the curved, black and white bridge. This charming part of the Weaver Valley sees hundreds of anglers at weekends, immersed in silent concentration. Downriver a flotilla of swans drifts under the viaduct of the Chester to Manchester railway line. Continue on the hardcore track until you come to Vale Royal Locks, part of the Weaver Navigation.

Brine springs on the banks upstream attracted the Romans, and by 1732 over 9,000 tons of rock salt and 5,000 tons of white salt were carried downstream annually. After several attempts, an Act of Parliament to canalise the river was passed; and in 1830 it was dredged to a depth of 7' 6" (2.5 metres), while locks 88 feet (28 metres) long were built to allow cargoes of up to 150 tons to be carried. The locks were widened to 42 feet (13 metres) in 1874.

**SJ 639705** Return over the arm of the old river, to Vale Royal drive and go back to the L, under dark, overhanging yews and hollies. Twenty-five yards (8 metres) on, a flight of shallow sandstone steps bordered by dense, viridian rhododendrons, climb up to the R. They're clearly marked by yellow arrows on a post. At the top of the short slope a stile leads out into open fields.

*A sandstone sarcophagus - the word means 'flesh-eater' - stands propped on boulders behind decaying Vale Royal House.*

Ahead, the path runs diagonally across undulating pasture to a distant line of trees.

**SJ 635701**  At the woods' edge, a quarter of a mile (0.5 km) later, climb over a stile and descend some crude steps into the shade of the trees. Here two paths cross. We go straight over. The path to the L

~~~~~~~~~~~~~~~~~~~~~~~~~~~~~~~~~~~~~~~~~~~~~~~~~~~~~~

leads back to Vale Royal drive, and though not an official public right of way, has been in use as such for years; while to the R the path leads to Rookery Pool, a 5 acre (2 hectare) fishing water, which once boasted a boathouse belonging to Vale Royal House.

These lovely open, deciduous woods are home to a wealth of birds and animals. Feral mink can sometimes be glimpsed nearer the river. Across a stream, the path winds through groves of straight beeches that are heavy with the scent of bluebells in early summer. Fallen trees, dips and hillocks add to the appeal of the place.

**SJ 634700** At the further edge of this narrow finger of woodland, another yellow-arrowed stile points out over the fields. The path runs straight across them, towards Vale Royal drive hidden under its avenue of tall beeches. At the top of Church Wood, 400 metres later, go L along the edge, beneath an unusual Turkey oak with its bristly-cupped acorns, to rejoin the stately avenue.

Opposite is the stile where we first launched out across the fields at the beginning of this circuit of the site of Vale Royal Abbey. Now we go R, back down the drive towards Whitegate village. Sweet chestnuts from the flanking trees cover the drive in autumn, and woodpigeons clatter away from the upper branches.

An oasis of green between Winsford and Northwich, Whitegate with its black and white cottages, its church, its maypole, its trees, its pools, parkland and river valley is still aptly named: it is still a "Vale Royal of England". And let us hope it stays that way.

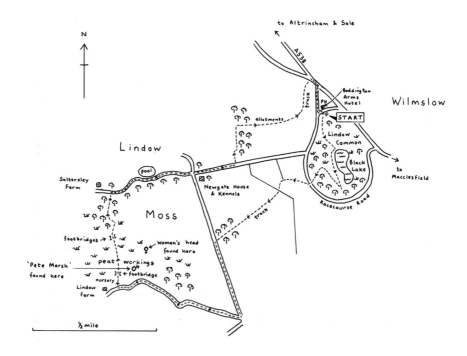

N

to Altrincham & Sale

A538

Boddington Arms Hotel

Wilmslow

PH

START

Lindow Common

Black Lake

to Macclesfield

allotments

track

Lindow

pool

Saltersley Farm

Newgate House & Kennels

Moss

track

Racecourse Road

footbridges →

Woman's head found here

'Pete Marsh' found here

peat workings

← footbridge

nursery

Lindow Farm

½ mile

**Lindow Moss**

# 11 Lindow Moss ~ *in search of the Bog Man* ~

**Lindow Common and Black Lake, Lindow Moss, peat cutters, giant vegetables, and two 'bog burials' - Iron Age sacrificial victims found preserved in the peat.**

**Start:** *Wilmslow, 10 miles (16 kilometres) south of Manchester. Map reference SJ 833814.*
**Distance:** *3.5 miles (5.5 kilometres).*
**Duration:** *2.5-3 hours.*
**Maps:** *OS 1:50,000 Landranger Sheet 118 Stoke-on-Trent and Macclesfield area; OS 1:25,000 SJ 88.*
**Terrain:** *Flat. Surfaced paths, lanes, sandy bridleways, peat bog and mossland. Wet and muddy in winter. Potentially dangerous for children and dogs.*
**Food and Drink:** *Boddington Arms Hotel, Altrincham Road, Wilmslow, opposite the car park at the northern end of Lindow Common. Map reference SJ 833817.*
*Tel: Wilmslow 525849.*

Lindow Moss is a sinister place. Dark forces lurk there still. Cross the bog on a winter's day scoured by horizontal rain, and the morass of peat diggings, black-water ditches, birch scrub and heathland evokes a distant past inhabited by earth deities, water spirits and the supernatural.

Even today Cheshire is rich in Celtic tradition: 'horsing' and 'soul-caking' are practised annually at Antrobus, sword and antler dances have their followers, stone heads are venerated yet. While the 'Old Religion' lives on the sophistication of the Electronic Age remains a thin veneer. And, as if to remind us of the proximity of this alien past, the naturally embalmed body of an Iron Age sacrificial victim was unearthed from the Moss in August 1984. Pickled by the peat, he was called the 'Bog Man' by archaeologists; while some wit from the Press dubbed him 'Pete Marsh'.

Meres, marshes and mosslands once covered large tracts of Cheshire. Little now remains, and that only in fragments. Lindow Moss was formed in two shallow hollows within the boulder clay and glacial gravels left behind after the last Ice Age. Originally it extended over 1,500 acres (600 hectares) in the shape of a ragged tea cosy. But by the 1840s the Moss had shrunk to only 750 acres (300 hectares), and today it covers only about 80 acres (32 hectares), half of which is now worked commercially for peat extraction.

**SJ 833814** Our walk begins on the eastern outskirts of Wilmslow, 10 miles (16 kms) south of Manchester city centre, at the northern tip of Lindow Common. Turn off the A538 Wilmslow to Altrincham road by the Boddington Arms Hotel, onto Racecourse Road. The road circles the Common. The large public car park opposite the hotel has ample parking space.

Here a Cheshire County Council board explains the history and management of Lindow Common. It's a local Nature Reserve and a Site of Special Scientific Interest (SSSI); and. careful control of the vegetation on a 3-6 year cycle makes sure that plants and animals like the bog asphodel and the now scarce common frog survive.

**SJ 834812** Out on the Common a web of paths spreads through the mixed birch, willow and heather scrub. Take the central of three paths, and at a five-way junction take the path second from the R, to emerge at Black Lake. Translated into Welsh, with its Celtic roots, this becomes *Llyn Ddu* - *llyn* means lake and *ddu* means black - the probable origin of the name Lindow.

Out on Lindow Moss - from the Celtic, 'llyn ddu' meaning black lake - narrow gauge tracks snake away over black and ancient peat formed long ago in the Iron Age marshes.

~~~~~~~~~~~~~~~~~~~~~~~~~~~~~~~~~~~~~~~~~~~~~~~~~~~

On the eastern edge of the peat bog, what is now the Common was once part of larger Lindow Moss. Pollen samples from peat deposited nearly two thousand years ago show that by late Roman times the woodland on the edge of the Moss had been cleared, and the area was a mixture of wasteland and pasture. And like 'wasteland' today, the Moss became a place on the margins of society, a place for the poor, the dispossessed, the outcast.

During the 1700s a shepherd became a well known figure on the Common; he carried a crook and wore low shoes with large buckles, knee breeches, a red waistcoat, a brown top coat and a round hat. But disastrous fires often swept the Common in dry summers, and a photograph from the 1890s shows the area as a sandy, treeless heath. Adders up to 14 inches (35 cms) long were common and a viper catcher came to trap them each year; in 1877 a boy was bitten whilst collecting bilberries.

In about 1771, Squire Finney, a local landowner and magistrate, persuaded two local lords to enclose much of the Moss; part of the rents raised was used to build a workhouse for the poor on the edge of the Common in 1773. Later the open ground was used for horse racing. Finally, in 1897 the Common was bought for a large sum by a local J.P., and presented to Wilmslow District Council on Queen Victoria's Diamond Jubilee.

At the Black Lake turn R on the broad, encircling path. Signs warn of thin ice, and mixed flocks of ducks and gulls sit in rafts out on the dark water. But if the heather and birch scrub evoke the past, the roar of taxiing jets preparing to take-off at nearby Manchester Airport are a salutary reminder of the present.

**SJ 834810** Beyond the last seat at the end of the lake, a path goes off to the R. Cross the next minor path and, 100 metres on, turn L towards the edge of the Common. Go through the wooden kissing gate and cross Racecourse Road.

**SJ 833810** Directly opposite is Lindow Lane - marked by a sign with

~~~~~~~~~~~~~~~~~~~~~~~~~~~~~~~~~~~~~~~~~~~~~~~~~~~~~

white letters on a green ground. This is the old margin of the Moss. Now the ponies of the rich graze on either side; but once the Moss was the last resort of the poor, where ordinary people had cut turves for the fire, collected firewood and grazed cows, pigs and ponies since time immemorial.

**SJ 830810** Within 250 metres of the road, by cream-painted Racecourse Farm, the potholed lane bends sharply to the L. Soon the narrow, unsurfaced track runs out across the Moss, past paddocks and ramshackle stables. The lane kinks around a secluded house and then heads on beneath a natural avenue of birches and young ash. Donkeys gaze from the field to the R, and there is scrub woodland to the L. Notice how the path is raised above them; drained for over a century, the Moss is shrinking, and settling back upon itself.

**SJ 827808** A little farther on, a second path runs back to the L; but we go straight on, through an ingenious gate-cum-stile designed to let only horses and people pass. Another 200 metres on, at a T-junction of paths, turn L onto a broad bridleway. Alder and sycamore fringe the path, now raised more obviously above the fields.

**SJ 827804** Squeeze past a second gate by a white house; the bridleway beyond is tarmaced. At the end of this metalled section two County Council' signs tell us this is 'Public Path 34' and the 'Bridle Path To Morley'. Continue on past Springfield Drive to the end of Rotherwood Road.

**SJ 827802** Then turn R, along clearly signed Moor Lane, past a row of houses built between the wars. Continue past 'Ned Yates' Garden Centre' and 'Moorland House'. From here a patchy tarmac road winds out past more houses into open farmland. A little farther on the lane passes 'Middlebrook Mushrooms' and 'Swan Plant Hire' on the R. Winter wheat pushes up in the large fields to the L, and harsh-voiced piebald magpies echo the black and white of Friesian cattle chewing the cud nearby.

**SJ 823802** At the end of a straight stretch of road the lane bends

~~~~~~~~~~~~~~~~~~~~~~~~~~~~~~~~~~~~~~~~~~~~~~~~~~~~~

sharply to the L. Around the corner is the entrance to 'Lindow Court Park' caravan site, while ahead are the orange, metal gates of 'Horticon' tree nursery. Turn R through a white latch-gate between the two. From here a limestone-chipping surfaced path runs alongside the nursery.

**SJ 819804** About 100 metres from the white latch-gate, go R, through a gap in the fence between two posts. The path cuts across the nursery between the serried ranks of thousands of young trees: ashes, beeches, sycamores and maples. They thrive in the moisture-retaining peat, and judging by the wealth of molehills, so do humus-digesting earthworms.

Beyond the narrow strip of the tree nursery, a concrete slab bridges a ditch cut deep into the black peat. A battered sign warns, *Danger - Peat Workings. Deep Ditches.* In the last century both men and cattle were drowned in the bog, which was wetter then. Though partially drained, these peat workings remain treacherous; dogs still drown in the vertically-sided ditches, and the solid appearance of the cut peat surface is often deceptive - step off the path and you could sink up to your waist, or worse. Be warned!

From here the path runs out across the Moss. To the L are the black spires of drying peat heaps, to the R an area of open heath colonised by sparse birches and heather. We are back in a landscape reminiscent of an older Cheshire, a landscape before forest clearance, agricultural drainage, and the patchwork of hedged fields that characterise the land today. Half-close your eyes, and this last fragment of the Moss grows in the imagination: dotted in the distant past with reed-rimmed pools, it is larger, wetter, silent and more dangerous. Water rails scream in the reed-beds like stuck pigs. It is an eerie fastness filled with menace. And beneath the surface of the pools Celtic boggarts and *bobodha* - or bogey-men - wait to pull the careless wanderer down into the black water.

From the Bronze Age onwards, prehistoric man no doubt fished and hunted here for eels, otters and wild ducks. The Moss was rich with opportunity; a place to be exploited even then. A Victorian writer mentions, *"what appeared to be a roadway made of logs of timber placed end to end, with sleepers across, laid close together, and this I am told continued for some length up the Moss".* This sounds very much like the prehistoric 'Sweet Track' found in the Somerset Levels (a similar ancient wetland) -  a primitive access road.

**SJ 819806** Walk on. Two hundred metres later, when the scrub area on the R ends,  the peat diggings open out on either side. Concealed beneath the dark surface here are often macabre relics of an unkind past. Bogs are peculiar in many ways. William King, the Archbishop of Dublin, wrote in 1685, *"that a Turf-Bog preserves things strangely, a Corps will ly entire in one for several years; I have seen a piece of leather pretty fresh dug out of a Turf-Bog, that had never in the memory of man been dug before."* At Burwell Fen, in East Anglia, the preserved body of a man was found upright in the peat in the position in which he had drowned. Dressed in a belted leather coat, he stood in a wooden dugout canoe, his arm still raised in a last gesture of horror. He died perhaps 2,500 years ago, back in the Iron Age. Even more bizarre is the unauthenticated account of a knight in full armour, still mounted on his horse, found in Solway Moss where, centuries before, a battle was fought in 1542. Choked in a nightmare mixture of mud and water, both died in terror to be preserved inadvertently for posterity.

But not all bodies preserved in the peat have died a natural death. Some have been  murdered, and others sacrificed in ritual killings.

# Lindow Woman And Lindow Man ~ The Bodies In The Bog

*In May 1983 two workmen discovered a round, peat covered object at the peat-packing plant on the edge of the Moss. It was soft and pliable and, as a joke, they called it a dinosaur's egg. But when they hosed it clean they saw it was a human skull, with traces of hair and flesh still attached.*

The police were called. A local man subsequently confessed to the murder of his wife, and was tried and convicted. Yet, ironically, the skull turned out to belong not to his wife's body, but to a woman who had died 2,500 years earlier, around 500 BC, back in the Iron Age. Despite careful searches, no other trace of the corpse was found; it seems likely that the head alone was buried in the bog as part of a Celtic ritual sacrifice.

A year later one of the same workmen pulled a well-preserved leg from the peat elevator. When archaeologists visited the Moss the next morning they discovered a flap of skin protruding from the uncut edge of the peat, not far from the site where the woman's skull had been buried. On excavation it turned out to be the ancient body of an Iron Age man pickled in the peat.

The lower half of the body was missing, cut off by the mechanical diggers. Tests showed the dead man had been about 25 years old, was fit and that his teeth were in good condition. He had a well-trimmed beard and moustache, and his manicured nails suggest he was probably a nobleman.

That this was a ritual killing is supported by his wounds. There was damage to the skull, around the neck was a twisted leather thong, and the throat had been slit; Lindow Man was first knocked unconscious, then slowly garotted, and lastly had his throat cut. In his preserved stomach were found traces of burnt bread and mistletoe, sacred to the Druids. It seems probable that he suffered the 'threefold death' referred to by the Roman chronicler, Lucan, as a sacrifice to a triad of powerful Celtic gods: Teutates, Esus and Taranis. The burnt bread and mistletoe were his last meal.

Lindow Moss may have been a grisly Iron Age votive site, a place of great sanctity in an ancient water cult. The bodies of other victims could well lie beneath the peat awaiting discovery.

*Looking out over Lindow Moss towards the area where the preserved bodies of both Lindow Man and Lindow Woman were discovered.*

**SJ 819808** Keep to the path. Soon two bridges made of baulks of timber and steel plate cross deep drainage ditches cut into the Moss. The water is an inky black and the sides are sheer; to fall in might well prove fatal. Between these parallel chasms is a narrow gauge railway used to haul the half-dried peat to the processing depot. Silver on black, it snakes away across the peat.

Two orange Hy-Macs - long-armed diggers - nowadays excavate

119

'rooms' in the peat, up to 200 metres long, 7 metres wide and a metre deep. But for centuries the peat was cut by hand. In the past it was used as fuel, not wantonly for gardens and horticultural big business, and so was cut in 'turves', or slabs. In the early 1900s one of the peat cutters was Old Jobie. He lived in a one-room shack out on the Moss, and could cut up to five thousand peats a week, for which he was paid £5.

Beyond the two bridges the path climbs into bracken and willow scrub. Go L at the top of the slope, curve around to the R, and cross a further bridge into a wood. The springy peat is replaced by sand underfoot, and we have temporarily left the Moss. Go straight ahead, through the narrow strip of woodland, and at the field boundary turn R away from Saltersley Farm.

**SJ 819809** The path leaves the wood 250 metres later, and crosses a stile into a field. Over a second stile the path emerges on a rough farm road, beneath tall horse chestnuts.

**SJ 820810** Go R, away from the farm. Past a collection of lean-tos and a gate, is a lake. A story in the local press tells how, a number of years ago, a man returned from abroad to find his favourite footpath submerged by this new pool, which was formed from an old sandpit. So, to the loud cheers of a crowd of onlookers, he swam across the lake in a wetsuit and flippers to join up the severed ends of his path. No wonder he got his picture in the paper!

Today the pool attracts fishermen from the 'Prince Albert Angling Society' of Macclesfield. Bream, roach, rudd, perch and pike mingle with a few hefty carp - the largest caught in 1988 weighed 18lb (8 kgs); just a smidgeon short of the British rod-caught record of 51lb (23 kgs)!

Past thickets of gorse, the track curves around the lake, and into the shade of birch, ash and oak woodland. Small brick and wood bungalows here are the descendants of squatters' homes shown built on the same spot on the 1843 Tithe Map of the area.

~~~~~~~~~~~~~~~~~~~~~~~~~~~~~~~~~~~~~~~~~~~~~~~~~~

**SJ 824810** Three hundred metres later, the track emerges on a metalled road. The bridle path to the R leads back to Moor Lane, but we go straight on beneath a sign that warns, '! - Animals. Slow'. Past 'Newgate House and Kennels', the road is raised once more above the peaty paddocks where ponies graze.

**SJ 827811** From here the road runs directly back to Lindow Common and the car park. But if, 350 metres on, you turn L through the gates of 'Newgate Disposal Site', the Moss still holds a few surprises. When lorries pass, the road shivers on its bed of spongy peat. Keep to the righthand edge of the landfill site; 350 metres on, a sign tells us this is the 'Borough of Macclesfield Public Footpath No. 96'. The undulating hills beyond are composed entirely of accumulated rubbish; perhaps 30 metres (100 feet) below this modern detritus is the black peat of the unwanted Moss.

**SJ 827814** At the sign, go R, down a flight of crude steps and into the primitive-looking woods. Within 100 metres is the make-do fence of the 'Lindow Horticultural Society's Members Gardens', or allotments. Look over the fence. A combination of peat, manure and hard work has produced vegetables on a gigantic scale: rhubarb with leaves like golfing umbrellas, parsley as big as gooseberry bushes, football-sized lettuces, house-high runner beans and leeks like alabaster table legs. It's a vegetarians' fantasy, or like something from a fairytale.

Beyond, the track runs on past large houses, and curves to the L by a row of cottages, to emerge on the main A 538 Altrincham to Wilmslow road. Turn R, alongside the busy road for 10 metres, and then go R again down a rough lane. When it ends, a little further on, turn L and then, almost immediately R, into the car park opposite the Boddington Arms Hotel.

After the brooding solitude and black foreboding of the Moss, Wilmslow's well-tended fringe seems almost tame. Yet, if the wild Moss should vanish altogether, it seems likely there will be secrets still hidden in the depths - of ancient sacrifice, dark rites and death.

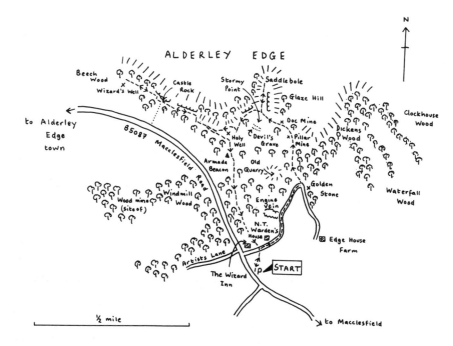

**Alderley Edge**

# 12 Alderley Edge ~ *across the Copper Hills* ~

Legend of the Wizard of Alderley Edge, Bronze Age copper mines, Stormy Point, Holy Well, Armada Beacon, sandstone caves and hidden mine entrances.

---

**Start**: *Alderley Edge, 12 miles (19 kilometres) south of Manchester. National Trust car park, on the B5087. Map reference* **SJ 860772**.

**Distance**: *3.5 miles (5.5 kilometres).*

**Duration**: *3 hours.*

**Maps**: *OS 1:50,000 Landranger Sheet 118, Stoke-on-Trent and Macclesfield area; OS 1:25,000 Sheet SJ 87.*

**Terrain**: *Fairly level, but with steep paths on slopes of Alderley Edge. Dry and sandy, muddy patches in winter.*

**Food and Drink**: *The Wizard Inn. Map reference* **SJ 860773**. *Restaurant and tea room. Tel: Alderley Edge 58400.*

---

Once upon a time, so the traditional Legend of Alderley Edge begins, a Mobberley farmer, crossing the Edge on his way to market to sell a white mare, is accosted by a wizard. Appearing from nowhere, the old man tells the farmer:

*"Thy horse is doomed to be,*
*Heir to a nobler destiny"*

Puzzled, at first the farmer refuses to part with the horse. But on his return, after a fruitless day at market, he readily agrees. The wizard leads the farmer, past a number of carefully mentioned places on the Edge, to the Iron Gates - a magical entrance to the underworld, concealed in the rock. There, deep in a cavern, he sees a circle of fully-armed warriors, each with a milk-white steed, lying in an enchanted sleep. They await some dark and future day when they will ride out to save England. But one warrior lies next to an empty space - he has no horse. At last the farmer understands. And so, in return for the horse, the wizard pays the farmer three times the animal's value, in treasure from a subterranean store.

Treasure? A subterranean store? Yes, for hidden within the legend are clues to real events; events in a distant past that were to shape the face of Cheshire. Perhaps such clues are older folk memories woven into traditional story form. Whatever their origin, the list of places named in the legend helps to illuminate Man's earliest search for metals which began some 4,000 years ago, back in the Bronze Age. Copper ore has long been mined underneath the Edge. The old mine workings: levels, adits, spoil heaps, smelting hearths and inclines, can still be traced today. The wizard's real treasure was the copper concealed beneath Cheshire's sandstone hills!

**SJ 860772** Our walk begins at the National Trust car park - just beyond The Wizard Inn, one mile (1.5 kms) east of Alderley Edge on the B 5087 Macclesfield road. There's plenty of space; and sometimes even an ice-cream van.

From the car park, take the short path that leads to The Wizard Country Restaurant; once a pub, it now has tea rooms and a 'National Trust Information Centre' behind. In 1938, 218 acres (90 hectares) of the Edge were bought by the Pilkington sisters with the help of Cheshire County Council, and later given to the National Trust.

**SJ 773801** Go R, down a sandy gravel drive, past 'Forester's Lodge' - the home of the Edge's National Trust warden. To the R are rolling fields and to the L mixed birch, oak, rowan and scots pine woodland. The Edge's trees are relatively new; until quite recently the hill could boast panoramic views around the compass. In prehistoric times, the Edge was a stretch of wild moorland spangled with boggy pools and thick with heather, furze and broom. But by 1640, beech trees, imported from the south, had been introduced to the estate by the landowner, Sir Thomas Stanley. And the first scots pines were planted only in 1745.

**SJ 861775**  Three hundred metres past the lodge, the woods open out to the L. Go through a gap in the fence between two posts. This is the Engine Vein, where a line of five early mining pits were excavated in around 1900. Twenty stone hammer-heads, a number of flint tools and the remains of a wooden spade - which was dated by the British Museum as Bronze Age - were found in the vicinity. Together, they point to extensive prehistoric mineral exploration.

From the Engine Vein, later galleries and levels reach out beneath the Edge; the total length of the underground workings from east to west is about 480 feet (146 metres), making them small in comparison with West and Wood Mines. Nonetheless, the area is protected as a Site of Special Scientific Interest, or SSSI. Today the workings are blocked off for the safety of the public.

*Shallow pits and the discovery of stone hammers near the Engine Vein Mine indicate probable Bronze Age working of this natural rock-fault.*

~~~~~~~~~~~~~~~~~~~~~~~~~~~~~~~~~~~~~~~~~~~~~~~~~~~~~~~~~~~~~~~~

# Alderley Edge Mines

"In the space of a few acres," *wrote an excited mineralologist, in 1811,* "are the ores of most of the metals found in England." *That is not quite true; but copper, lead, iron, zinc, silver, arsenic, silicon, barium, vanadium and magnesium are all found, in a bewildering variety of forms. Most occur as thin films coating the pebbles and grains of the porous sandstone. Crystals are rare: only at the Engine Vein have small, cubic crystals of galena - or lead - been found.*

*Alderley Edge was created millions of years ago, when a huge block, or horst, of sandstone was pushed up between two faults. Warm, saline solutions carrying dissolved metals then percolated up the faults and out into the surrounding rock. They are not igneous intrusions. Even at this moment minerals are being redeposited on the mine surfaces; it's a continuous process.*

*Four thousand years ago, Bronze Age miners were attracted to this then desolate ridge by the brightly-coloured copper ores that stained the surface. They extracted the ores from lines of pits along the faults. Some sources suggest the Romans worked the copper ore and lead too. But no evidence survives; nor is there any reference in Domesday. The hills were quiet until the seventeenth century. Between 1693 and 1879, seven different mining concerns tried their luck. Some, like The Copper Mining Company of Macclesfield, made their fortunes. Others were ruined. Then, in 1807 the mines were revitalised by the discovery of cobalt - used to give the blue tint to porcelain, and rare in Britain. The mines were re-opened briefly in 1865 to provide magnesium and vanadium for the experiments of Sir Henry Roscoe FRS; and again during the 1914-18 war.*

*Victorian visitors were once enthralled by passages and caverns lit by guides with candles, flares and fireworks. But after a spate of fatalities, the last entrances were finally sealed off in 1964 by 'Blaster' Bates, the explosives expert and raconteur, using 224 sticks of gelignite.*

~ ~ ~ ~ ~ ~ ~ ~ ~ ~ ~ ~ ~ ~ ~ ~ ~ ~ ~ ~ ~ ~ ~ ~ ~ ~ ~ ~ ~ ~ ~ ~ ~ ~ ~ ~ ~ ~ ~ ~ ~

**SJ 863776** Return to the drive and turn L. Two hundred metres on, at a meeting of paths, the drive sweeps to the R towards Edge House Farm. A large boulder by the side of the track here is the Golden Stone, mentioned in the legend of the Wizard; perhaps it had some significance to the prehistoric miners. The path ahead leads to secluded Clockhouse Wood and Dickens Wood, but we turn L, along the Edge, between the posts of a massive wooden fence designed to keep out cars and horses.

The woods here are alive with squirrels and jays. Beneath the trees take the right-hand fork, along the wider of the two paths, marked as being suitable for wheelchairs.

**SJ 862777** Fifty metres on, branch R again, down beside a wired off plantation of young beech trees. The narrow path dips slightly downhill until it comes to the lip of the Edge.

As the fence angles away upslope, go R, down some crude wooden steps. The path descends the curve of the slope beneath tall scots pines, to emerge on a bare sandy hillside, where a jumble of sandstone blocks spill out from the Edge.

**SJ 862778** Carved into the red-, yellow- and white-striated rock-face is the cave-like entrance to Pillar Mine. It dates from around 1780. A pillar of sandstone stood at the entrance until late summer 1975, when it was demolished by vandals. Inside the entrance, the stone is blackened with the soot of fires, and strange symbols have been carved into the soft rock: Alderley Edge has long attracted rumours of witchcraft, especially at Halloween. Beyond the 'cave', a low-ceilinged tunnel, or level, extends into the darkness for 100 feet (30 metres) to open out in a small chamber, from which further passages spread out like fingers from a hand. The entrance to a second, lower level, which runs much farther under the Edge, has since been blocked by soil sliding down the hill into the 'cave' mouth. The way in is now buried under the west side of the floor.

From Pillar Mine, continue obliquely up the slope to the L, over large sandstone boulders and bare sandy slopes. At the top once more, the path opens out onto Stormy Point.

**SJ 861780** One of the better known parts of Alderley Edge, Stormy Point rises 300-400 feet (90-120 metres) above the Cheshire Plain. On a clear day the view encompasses the Derbyshire hills and parts of greater Manchester; below, black and white Friesian cattle look like toys spread out in the geometric, emerald-green fields.

Back from the edge is a narrow, slot-like excavation known as the 'Devil's Grave'. Walk down the cleft and below an overhang is a broad, sloping cave, filled with leaves, branches and rubbish. A circular hole in the roof has been wisely covered with a hefty stone block. The Stormy Point fault runs across the sandy ground due south of a memorial whose plaque reads: *These woods were given to the National Trust in memory of Lawrence Pilkington and Mary Pilkington who enjoyed the walks and wide views.* Several small trial workings have been made east of the 'Devil's Grave'.

*From the cave-like entrance to Pillar Mine a tunnel extends 30 metres into the Upper Mottled Sandstone, to open out in a small chamber.*

From the memorial, a path leads off to the R, towards Saddle Bole. As

~~~~~~~~~~~~~~~~~~~~~~~~~~~~~~~~~~~~~~~~~~~~~~

it drops gently downhill, along the contours of the slope, curious slabs of rock, like teeth, jut from the ground; and tall, majestic beeches stretch 80-100 feet (25-30 metres) up to the light. If their green-grey trunks are like muscled sinews, then in contrast their exposed roots are like arthritic fingers, clutching at the earth. Numerous trial shafts, levels and pits dot the crest of Glaze Hill, along the fault; and these excavations are regarded as among the oldest in the Alderley Edge area.

**SJ 860781**  Two hundred metres from the memorial, at the end of Glaze Hill, is the pitted summit of Saddle Bole. The first part of the name comes from an old saddle-road that climbed the hill at this point, while 'bole' was the old name for a wind-driven smelter. As early as the 1690s, trees and gorse from the wooded slopes were used to fuel crude smelting hearths, which caught the prevailing westerly winds up on this exposed hill.

**SJ 860779**  Return to Stormy Point and turn R at the memorial. Across the open ground, two paths move back into the trees. Take the path that drops obliquely down a gentle slope, not the flatter, broader one marked for wheelchairs. Roots and outcrops of rock jut from the surface as the path runs downhill.

**SJ 859778**  A hundred metres down the slope, two paths cross. Turn R, downhill again, on a new, timber-edged path, that crosses a narrow stream on a stone slab. The path curves around the side of a steep slope, beneath oaks, hollies and dark yews. A little farther on, water drops constantly down a damp, mossy rock face and into a slab-sided stone trough. Just around the corner is a second, oval trough, this time carved from one piece of sandstone; water trickles into it from a groove cut in the overhang above. This is the Holy Well. It's an attractive spot; the trough and cave behind sheltered beneath two vast beech trees. Behind the trough, in the rock face, is the supposed site of the Iron Gates where, in the legend, the wizard and the farmer entered the underworld. Even as little as a century ago there were people still living who swore they had seen the Iron Gates and that they were real!

Scots pines as straight as ships' masts line the slopes as the path crosses a crude log bridge, kinks sharply to the R, and climbs steeply up a flight of timber-edged steps.

**SJ 857777** At the crest of the slope turn R at a T-junction, and follow the well-used path along the top of the Edge. The shelved outcrops of barites-rich sandstone 50 metres on are supposed to show the outlines of the Wizard's footprints - an example of the growth of the popular legend to embrace almost everything on the Edge.

**SJ 856777** Within another 100 metres the path opens out once more at Castle Rock. Perhaps the most visited part of the Edge, Castle Rock was the site originally chosen in 1225 by the sixth Earl of Chester, Ranulph de Blundeville, for a castle. But though the area was levelled, the castle was re-sited at Beeston Crag, 25 miles (40 kms) to the south-east.

From Castle Rock continue on the path alongside the fence. A few yards later, at a junction of paths, don't turn L towards the road, but R, between two stone posts and down a short flight of steps. At the bottom turn L, on a path along the contour of the slope.

**SJ 855781** Sandstone bluffs overhang the path; beneath the first are the remains of a Victorian bench, the panoramic view from which is now obscured by oaks and scrub elder. Further outcrops border the path; 100 metres on, as the path starts to dip downhill beyond a bend, is the Wizard's Well. Shaded by beech and holly trees, the well is nothing more than a simple stone trough into which water drips from the mossy stone above. What makes it unusual is the legend carved into the stone: *Drink of this, and take thy fill, for the water falls by the Wizard's will.* Trace the letters with your fingers.

Return to the bottom of the stone steps, and continue on the path that skirts the base of Castle Rock. The path winds along the contour of the slope, keeping close to the sandstone bluff. Look at the different coloured strata.

~~~~~~~~~~~~~~~~~~~~~~~~~~~~~~~~~~~~~~~~~~~~~~~~

When the bluff ends, 250 metres later, the path climbs up the slope to the R, and rejoins the wider path along the top of the Edge. Turn L, and continue past the steps that dip down towards the Holy Well. Soon, a neatly walled off area belonging to the Water Board, appears on the R.

**SJ 858777**   At the far corner of the wall turn R, up a shallow flight of crude steps. At the top is a natural mound surmounted by a plaque. This is the Beacon. Six-hundred-and-fifty feet (200 metres) above sea-level, for years it stood out above the trees on the western edge of the woods. The Beacon appears on Saxton's early map of Cheshire, in 1577; and no doubt it was used to signal to the Helsby, Frodsham and Halton (Runcorn) beacons the coming of the Spanish Armada in 1588. Later, in 1779 a square building was built to house a vast iron pot full of pitch that could be lit at a moment's warning. But in 1931, on a windy December night the already rickety building was blown down!

From the Beacon go straight on, downhill, on a broad path. At the bottom of the slope, close to a second corner of the Water Board wall, take the broader, lefthand fork of the path; it's smoothly surfaced and again marked as suitable for wheelchairs. It leads back to the Wizard Restaurant, tea rooms and National Trust car park alongside the B5087.

But before you drive away, pause to consider the secret world hidden beneath your feet. Deep under the Edge the ancient tunnels snake away in the darkness. Connected by a twisted logic, these galleries, shafts and levels create an often deadly three dimensional maze. Now the only ways in are those made by the Derbyshire Caving Club. The underworld was never for the public; and so today, steel man-hole covers replace the Wizard's Iron Gates.

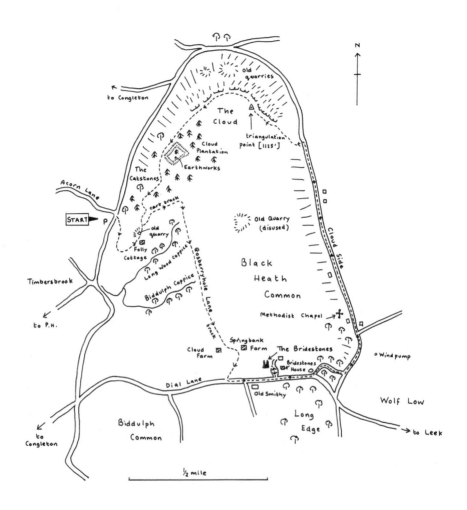

N

to Congleton

old quarries

The Cloud

Cloud Plantation

triangulation point [1125']

Earthworks

The Catstones

Acorn Lane

cart track

old quarry

START

P

Folly Cottage

Long Wood Coppice

Old Quarry (disused)

Gooseberryhole Lane

Black Heath Common

Cloud Side

Timbersbrook

Biddulph Coppice

to P.H.

Methodist Chapel

Springbank Farm

The Bridestones

Cloud Farm

Bridestones House

o Wind pump

Dial Lane

Old Smithy

Wolf Low

to Congleton

Biddulph Common

Long Edge

to Leek

½ mile

**Congleton**

# 13 Congleton ~ to the Bridestones and the Cloud ~

**Packhorse route, Biddulph Common, ancient green lane, Bridestones Neolithic burial chamber, oldest Primitive Methodist chapel, panoramic views from the Cloud.**

**Start:** *Cloudside, Timbersbrook, 3 miles (5 kilometres) east of Congleton. Map reference* **SJ 897630.**

**Distance:** *4.5 miles (7 kilometres).*

**Duration:** *3 hours.*

**Maps:** *OS 1:50,000 118 Stoke-on-Trent & Macclesfield area; OS 1:25,000 SJ 86 and SJ 96.*

**Terrain:** *Two steep ascents, otherwise easy. Old track, grass verge, quiet lane, sandy paths, upland moor and rocky paths. Muddy in places.*

**Food and Drink:** *Coach and Horses Inn, Under Rainow Road, Timbersbrook. Map reference* **SJ 890618.** *Robinsons. Friendly family atmosphere. Bar snacks 12-2, coffee. Tel: Congleton 273019.*

The Bridestones, a megalithic burial chamber high on Cheshire's eastern flank, is the oldest monument in the county. Revered and untouched until the 18th century, it has acted as a territorial marker for over 4,000 years; today it still guards the boundary between Cheshire and Staffordshire. Would such lasting significance have surprised its builders? We can only guess.

Five thousand years ago the climate was warmer. And the hills we now know as The Cloud, Congleton Edge and Mow Cop were grassy islands rising out of a flatland of marsh and densely wooded river valleys. By around 3500 BC pressure for easily cultivatable land on Europe's

133

~~~~~~~~~~~~~~~~~~~~~~~~~~~~~~~~~~~~~~~~~~~~~~~~~~~~~

western seaboard had grown to such a pitch that large numbers of colonists were sailing for Britain. These Neolithic people were farmers - part of an Agricultural Revolution that was an important step towards civilisation - and they slowly replaced the native hunter-gatherers. Britain's virgin land was fertile and there was ample room for expansion. Looking for light, upland soils that would need little clearing, the Neolithic immigrants moved inland up rivers and along the open ridges of the hills.

One such route brought travellers, perhaps via Ireland and the Isle of Man, to the prehistoric ford across the Mersey at Warrington, and so along the Knutsford Ridge and Alderley Edge to Congleton Cloud. Here they discovered the soils were right, there was a spring nearby and they settled. The rest is prehistory!

**SJ 897630** Our walk begins 650 feet (200 metres) up, at the bottom of Gosberryhole Lane, on Cloud Side, 2 miles (3 kms) east of Congleton. Park alongside the broad but quiet road. Cloud Side lane hugs the contours of the slope, and cuts across an older lane rising up from Congleton: on one side of the road it is called Acorn Lane, on the other Gosberryhole Lane.

Gosberryhole Lane is rough and unmetalled. Scots pine, rowan and hawthorn line the steep banks, and the lane climbs steadily, curving up to the R. Above is a large house, backed by a tower-like block of stone which juts from the Cloud's edge. Underfoot the modern limestone chippings are eroded in places to show worn gritstone cobbles. The lane is old, and crossed the hills avoiding the boggy ground to the south at Mossley- and Congleton Mosses.

**SJ 897628** As the lane jerks to the L around a sharp dogleg, bilberries and purple heather swathe the banks. The view opens out to the south along Congleton Edge; and to the R are the first glimpses of the broad panorama of the Cheshire Plain spread out below.

Soon the lane levels out and passes luxurious Folly Cottage with its stables and ornamental waterfowl. Nearby, on the L, is the deep, scrub and nettle filled chasm of a disused quarry. The track narrows, becomes rougher, and climbs again. Worn by the rain, outcrops of gritstone poke through the sandy path.

**SJ 898630** Beyond Folly Cottage, the path forks. Here a cast metal sign decorated with a green-painted oak-leaf cluster, announces: '*The National Trust. The Cloud. No Horses Please.* '

But we go R, on along Gosberryhole Lane, which levels out to follow the contours of the hill. In autumn the scene presents a vibrant tricolour of gold, green and blue: golden bracken and oaks on the rising slopes of The Cloud, a sky the blue of a gas-jet, and emerald rain-watered fields below. Crescented, modern hoofprints in the sandy soil remind us that this lane once saw packhorses, carts and travellers on foot ascending the hill. Look for the large slabs of gritstone laid into the track, a primitive road surface.

A well-made drystone wall, capped with round-topped stones, edges the lane to the L. Above is the dark line of Cloud Fir Plantation, shown on the 1841 Tithe Map. In those days the fields to the R were pastures only recently enclosed from wasteland.

**SJ 901631** A little farther on the lane bends sharply to the R. In Victorian times the field in the crook of the track was called Little Gooseberry Hall. But what are now open fields above the lane to the L, where cattle graze today, was still Black Heath Common (an uncultivated waste) in 1841. Even so, it wasn't wholly unused; the remains of another, larger quarry can be seen on the slopes.

For the next half-a-mile (1 km) the lane curves gently along the contour of the slope. A donkey brays from a distant farm, and a train rattles over the railway viaduct far below. Tall oak, beech and sycamore line the lane, and pale bramble shoots wave out over the track. To the R two streams, cut deep into the hillside, fall away downslope. Now an unruly tangle, the trees along both were once coppiced - cut for timber and then encouraged to shoot again. They were known as Long Wood Coppice and Biddulph Coppice; and both

135

~~~~~~~~~~~~~~~~~~~~~~~~~~~~~~~~~~~~~~~~~~~~~~~~~~~~~~~

belonged to a farmer with the richly Victorian-sounding name of Jeremiah Ginders!

**SJ 902625** The lane passes a small, walled off copse of sycamores and beeches around a black, leaf-mould filled pond. A fast trickle of water in the ditch to the R supports clumps of alien, indian balsam with its sweet smell of decay. The scent is cloying, if faint, and matches the large, mauve, orchid-like flowers.

As the lane bends uphill it is interesting to compare the two adjacent farms. One, evocatively-named Cloud Farm, is now a white-painted, double-garaged country retreat; the other, Springbank Farm, is a grey stone, working farm, surrounded by the day-to-day detritus of agriculture: dung heaps, timber, obselete hayrakes, milk churns and a collection of ramshackle corrugated-iron sheds in an abstract mixture of zinc, black and rust-red.

**SJ 904622** From Springbank Farm a drive stretches 200 metres to join the main road. The view back to the west encompasses a 120 degree panorama of Cheshire. Imagine how many thousands of pairs of eyes have scanned the view; and think too of how that view has altered.

**SJ 903621** At the road turn L, uphill, keeping to the broad grass verge. This is Dial Lane, once known as Dialstone Lane. In 1762, soon after Congleton's first silk mill opened, a group of merchants and landowners got together to form a turnpike company for the improvement of the Congleton-Leek-Ashbourne road to the important silk centre of Derby. The work was made cheaper by an Act of Parliament which granted rights, *"... to take furze, heath, stones, gravel, and sand [from] any Commons or Waste Grounds ... without paying anything."* In return for keeping the road in good repair, the company was allowed to erect toll bars to collect tolls. In 1804 the fee for a score of cattle or sheep was 5 pence, and for a wagon with wide wheels, 4 shillings. Farmers, funeral parties and the post paid nothing.

Past narrow Pines Lane is a diminutive cottage with sky-blue shutters, and damson trees in the wind-swept garden. Perhaps the view compensates for the bleak position.

**SJ 906621** Turn L, 150 metres from the cottage, between the massive gritstone gateposts of *'Bridestones Estate Farm.'* It's a private drive which gives access to the Bridestones. To the R of the drive, the sturdy stone wall is topped by rhododendrons and curious 'gothick' rockeries built of massive stones. Before the farm with its apocryphal notice warning, *'Beware of Bulls'*, turn L through a gate beneath dark yews.

## *The Bridestones*

*When the Bridestones Neolithic burial chamber was still new, sometime between 2900-2300 BC, it was an impressive mound over 300 feet (100 metres) long and 40 feet (12.5 metres) wide, enclosing not only the chamber visible today, but also two lateral chambers which were removed in the 18th century.*

*The 18 feet (6 metres) long central chamber was originally partitioned by an upright slab in which was cut a circular 'porthole'; today sadly only the lower half remains. Both the central and side chambers would originally have been roofed over with stone slabs. These megalithic - or 'large stone' - chambers were then covered by a mound of rocks, rubble and earth to form a long cairn.*

*The two large uprights were part of a curved facade that framed the entrance. In front of this daunting door to the underworld was a horned, semi-circular, paved forecourt, where pre-burial rites were conducted. Of the facade only three stones remain today; but an account of 1766 tells us that two centuries ago there were,"..* six or eight upright stones, from three to six feet broad, of various heights and shapes, fixed about six feet from each other in a semicircular form, and two stones within where the earth is very black from being mixed with ashes of oak-charcoal. It is apprehended that the circle was originally complete and 27 feet in diameter, for there is the appearance of holes where stones have been."

*Like other monumental cairns, the Bridestones was more than just a burial chamber; it was also a territorial marker, and the collective repository for the clan ancestors - rather like a family vault. Although excavations at the Bridestones in 1936-7 revealed only a small flint blade and scraper, but no bones, evidence from contemporary tombs shows they were often used over a very long period. Nor were whole bodies interred; rather selective bones, particularly femurs and skulls, were placed inside after the body had been allowed to decay naturally. Later burial customs included cremation. Only after long use were the tombs sealed up and covered with earth. Manipulation of the dead emphasised the continuity of clan lineage through the ancestors, and so helped to legitimise land use and tenure.*

*Though they were people much like us, our distant ancestors' view of the world was often one that we would find quite alien.*

So what happened to the cairn? Neolithic burial chambers had been revered by country people for millennia; but when the turnpike was built in 1762 the Company plundered several hundred tons of stone from the tomb, which stood conveniently on *"any Commons or Wastegrounds."* Much of the cairn material now lies under Dial Lane; the rest was incorporated into the artificial caves and 'Gothick' rockeries of Bridestones House, alongside the drive. Only a handful of large stones removed to Victoria Park, Tunstall, were returned in 1937.

From the Bridestones, return to the road, and turn L, uphill, past high-Victorian Bridestones House set in its landscaped shrubberies. Through the pillared gateway, inside the encircling stone walls, cedars, pampas grass and dark rhododendrons create an air of foreboding. Sheltered from the prevailing winds, it's a hidden, hilltop world. Beyond the house, the road continues uphill for 250 metres beside a holly hedge. At the top, where the road crosses the ridge at a slight saddle, an ancient, leaning signpost points back to 'Congleton' and on, over the brow, to 'Rushton and Leek'.

Two massive uprights are all that remain of the crescentic forecourt of the Bridestones
Neolithic long barrow. Behind them is the burial chamber for ritual deposition of the clan
dead.

139

~~~~~~~~~~~~~~~~~~~~~~~~~~~~~~~~~~~~~~~~~~~~~~~~~~~~~~~

**SJ 909621** Turn L, around the curve of the wall, onto a quieter side road. A scrubby wood of young birch and sycamore beside the lane shelters a dark, circular pool; and heather and bilberries cover the rough, irregular ground under young oaks. Shortly, the lane emerges on the far side of the ridge, on Staffordshire's Cloudside. Off to the R is the site of Wolf Low, a Bronze Age tumulus, or burial mound.

**SJ 910621** But we turn L. Look out over the drystone wall at another, quite un-Cheshire-like landscape: the hills and farms of the Peaks are more open, bleaker and less kind, yet with their own different charm.

For the next mile (1.5 kms) our route follows the contour of the ridge, along quiet Cloudside road. Beyond gritstone Willowshaw Farm nestled in the lee of the ridge, the road curves to the L, past a minor road signposted to 'Woodhouse Green'. Ahead, the view embraces the curious, truncated cone of Shutlingsloe and the massive concrete finger of Sutton Common transmission tower - designed to be proof against the vagaries of both war and civil unrest.

**SJ 910624** Tucked under the edge, up to the L, is Beech Tree Cottage with its proud vegetable gardens; at the end of each row of runner beans, in summer, is a 15 feet (5 metres) tall sunflower, waving in the sun. Behind the cottage is 'Cloud Methodist Chapel - Divine Worship Sundays - All Welcome'. It's now the oldest surviving Primitive Methodist chapel in use in England. In the early 1800s a group split away from the established Methodist church. Because they believed in conversion by praying and talking, local people called them 'The Ranters'. Tradition says the money for this chapel was raised in three days in 1815. Inside are oak pews and a simple pulpit with two brass candlesticks. The small, yellow brick extension was added in 1958.

From the chapel walk on past Willow Cottage and Lords Acre, among others, to Greenacres Farm, where two minah birds in an outdoor aviary whistle, cackle and call to passers-by. Go on past Cloudside Shooting Grounds and a ramshackle working farm, until the road narrows at a short rise.

140

Looking west from the Cloud, a plate-sized pool in the rock echoes the dark line of the cloud Fir Plantation in the distance.

~~~~~~~~~~~~~~~~~~~~~~~~~~~~~~~~~~~~~~~~~~~~~~~~~~~~

**SJ 907636** Before the lane drops downhill around the northern end of the Cloud, turn L up a track beside a parking space for 6-8 cars. A sign announces, 'Private Drive - Public Footpath Only - Please Do Not Obstruct'; and beneath it is a section of the 1:2,500 map showing the footpath - which is part of the 'Staffordshire Way'.

Just 25 metres from the road, the drive kinks L. Soon afterwards, follow the yellow arrow over a stile and up a flight of concrete steps to 'Cloud Summit'. At the top a narrow path emerges on open, windswept heather moor; the sense of space is exhilarating. No wonder then that beneath the conventional National Trust sign there is now another that pleads: 'No Hang-gliding'. The bracing air makes even adults want to fly.

**SJ 905637** The woody scent of heather rises from the moor even on the windiest of days. A white gritstone-sand covered path snakes uphill to the bleached concrete OS triangulation point; surveyors use these fixed points to calculate heights and distances across the country. The view, too, makes one pause as it spans the compass: the Peaks, Manchester, the Cheshire Plain, the Shropshire hills, Wales and the Mersey are all visible, stretched out like a map.

Beyond the triangulation (or 'trig') point, slablike outcrops of gritstone loom out over space at the end of the Cloud; while meadow pipits flit low over the heather, at home in their upland habitat. The houses, barns, trees and roads far below all look like toys; and the distant barking of two widely separated dogs echoes up from the plain.

**SJ 900635** From this rocky eyrie a path follows the edge down into the trees. At the boundary of the pine plantation the dominant heather of the tops changes to bilberries and fountains of tall grass. Soon the path levels and runs along the rim of the slope, hemmed in by a dark wall of close-ranked conifers. Here, on a spur facing south-west at 900 feet (280 metres), is what was once thought to be an Iron Age hillfort; but because of its regular rectangular shape and the feeble nature of its single bank and ditch, it is now considered to be a much later forestry enclosure.

~~~~~~~~~~~~~~~~~~~~~~~~~~~~~~~~~~~~~~~~~~~~~~~~~

**SJ 899632** The trees change from pines to softer oaks. When the path emerges at a junction of five ways, go R, slightly downhill. Soon the path broadens and bends sharply to the L and, almost immediately, to the R. A hundred metres later the water-worn path rejoins Gosberryhole Lane by the National Trust sign above Folly Cottage. Go straight on, downhill past Folly Cottage and so back to the bottom of Gosberryhole Lane and Cloudside.

Having circled the Cloud, it's easy to understand the attraction of the area. And to see, perhaps, why our distant forebears, the Neolithic builders of the Bridestones, should have chosen to live here, up on these breezy hills.

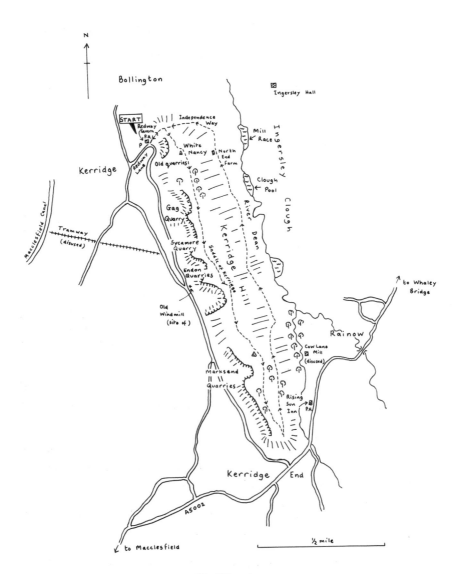

N

Bollington

Ingersley Hall

START
Redway
Tavern
P.H.
P
Redway Lane

Kerridge

Independence
Way

White
Nancy
Old quarries

North
End
Farm

Mill
Race

Clough
Pool

Ingersley Clough

Macclesfield Canal

Tramway
(disused)

Gag
Quarry

Sycamore
Quarry

Endon
Quarries

Kerridge Hill

Saddle of Kerridge

River Dean

to Whaley
Bridge

Old
Windmill
(site of)

Rainow

Cow Lane
Mill
(disused)

Marksend
Quarries

Rising
Sun
Inn
P.H.

Kerridge End

to Whaley
Bridge

A5002

to Macclesfield

½ mile

**Bollington**

# 14 Bollington ~ from 'White Nancy' along Kerridge Ridge ~

'White Nancy', beacon site, Kerridge Stone quarries, fossils, Peaks and plains, derelict mill, coal pits and flag-stoned footpath.

---

**Start:** *Kerridge near Bollington, 3 miles (5 kilometres) north-east of Macclesfield. Map reference **SJ 937772**.*
**Distance:** *3 miles (5 kilometres).*
**Duration**: *3 hours.*
**Maps:** *OS 1:50,000 118 Stoke-on-Trent & Macclesfield area; OS 1:25,000 SJ 97.*
**Terrain:** *High wind-swept ridge, steep climb and descent, otherwise easy. Grassy paths along ridge, fields, bridleway. Muddy in parts but mainly dry.*
**Food and Drink:** *Redway Tavern, Windmill Lane, Kerridge. Map reference **SJ 937772**. Open all day Sunday. Food, families welcome, free children's entertainment.*
*Tel: Bollington 73591.*

---

Hard stone and soft cotton have shaped the history of Kerridge and her big sister, Bollington. Kerridge stone has been recognised since the beginning of the 16th century; while Bollington cotton rose to prominence only much later, from 1800 onwards.

Back in Tudor times, by the early 1500s over half of what was still called Macclesfield Forest had been enclosed: farms, sheepfolds and fields had been walled off in the valleys and on the lower slopes of the hills. "*Robert Shrigley*", a contemporary document tells us, "*hath taken in some intakes on the King's commyn called Caroyge [Kerridge] ... and builded a house and a chamber*". Such colonisation of 'waste' was officially encouraged. By 1515 the Crown had leased the stone rights to Macclesfield Corporation, and stone flags from the quarries were used *"to pave all the streets in the Town"*. Later the haphazard pitting of the common became dangerous. Quarrying was regulated; and in 1625 the leases were assigned to local landowners. The pale yellow sandstone has been prized ever since: many of Cheshire's older buildings are roofed with it - like Pott Shrigley' and Siddington' churches, and Prestbury's Priest's House ; while the nave of Christchurch, Oxford is paved with Kerridge stone.

King cotton came later. The soft water flowing from the porous gritstones and sandstones, together with wool from the hills, meant that spinning and weaving had long been important cottage industries in the area. But when water-driven machinery began to arrive in the 18th century, mills sprang up to replace the local craftsmen. From an essentially agricultural community of 1,200 inhabitants in 1801, Bollington had grown by 1851 to become a small industrial town of 4,600 people. In fact, so many skilled Lancashire workers moved in that Bollington was described as, *"a Derbyshire town in Cheshire peopled by Lancashire folk"*. The town mills weathered a slump when the supply of raw cotton dried up in 1861-65, during the American Civil War. Only to suffer when large numbers of Bollington people emigrated to Canada in the 1870s, attracted by newspaper advertisements offering assisted-passages and government land-grants. Spurred on by low wages and poor prospects, the numbers leaving had grown to a flood by 1911 - a movement halted only by the coming of the First World War. Today the mills, many of which are listed buildings, are used for other things.

**SJ 937772**   Our walk begins in Kerridge, just south of Bollington and 2 miles (3 kms) north-east of Macclesfield. Park close to white-painted Redway Tavern where Redway Lane loops sharply uphill in a hairpin bend to become Windmill Lane. Because it stands literally at the north end of Kerridge Ridge, the area is known as Northend. Like the nearby Bull's Head, Redway Tavern was bought, together with a few acres of rough grazing, by local Heaver's Brewery in 1905; in those days publicans often supplemented their income with part-time farming. Both

~~~~~~~~~~~~~~~~~~~~~~~~~~~~~~~~~~~~~~~~~~~~~~~~~~~~~~

pubs, too, were popular with Kerridge quarrymen; and both were sometimes the scene of inquests into the accidental deaths of quarry workers.

The row of five cottages next to the pub was known as *'Tuppence Ha'penny Row',* presumably because the rent of each at one time was a halfpenny a week.

From the ample pub car park a public footpath leads uphill to the R, beneath a tunnel of wild-cherry and sycamore trees. Now surfaced with concrete, the steep lane was once called Betty's Brew. At the top of the slope the lane bends to the R, crosses a cattle grid, and levels out on Independence Way.

**SJ 938773** The track leads on to Northend Farm, but instead we climb steeply up to the R. A four-way signpost points out the walkers' options. Outcrops of Kerridge Stone jut from the grassy slope, alongside some of the older quarries on the ridge. This is the steepest ascent of the whole walk, and is sometimes muddy.

**SJ 939771** But the sight of one of Cheshire's most curious landmarks looming over the brow of the ridge, draws the climber upward. 'White Nancy', as the monument is known, has been variously described as a sugar-loaf (sugar was once sold in large, pointed lumps), as a bishop's mitre, and as a lady in a long white cloak. It is said to stand on the site of a far older beacon. Built of white-washed stone, the monument was erected by the Gaskell family of nearby Ingersley Hall early in the nineteenth century to commemorate the Battle of Waterloo. Originally it was a kind of drystone summerhouse with a door and a stone table and circular bench inside. Squire Gaskell left two shillings and sixpence per year to white-wash the beacon. But constant vandalism meant that the doorway was eventually walled up.

A more interesting version of how 'White Nancy' got its name appears in a Victorian guide. John Gaskell apparently had the beacon built to guide home one of his brothers who had gone abroad. When the stonemason, a Mr Dod, had completed the work, his employer invited him to toast the structure. Dod downed his brandy and then recited a poem:

> *"Here's to the Mountain of Nancy,*
> *That's built upon Ingersley Hill,*
> *Here's good health, wealth and fancy,*
> *And give Dod another gill."*

Many of the Gaskell family' ladies were called Nancy - a popular name at the time.

*High on the northern end of wind-blown Kerridge Ridge stands the curious folly of White Nancy, built to commemorate the battle of Waterloo.*

White Nancy soon became a symbol for Bollington. Bonfires were lit on the hilltop near the Nancy to celebrate Queen Victoria's jubilees in 1887 and 1897; and to mark the coronations of Edward VII in 1902 and George V in 1911. A far bigger fire was caused by accident in the summer of 1911. After a long drought, the gorse was set alight one Sunday evening, and flames leapt high into the air, illuminating the ridge. The next morning revealed that little actual damage had been done; but the free spectacle was long remembered.

The view from the monument is impressive too; which isn't surprising at 290 metres (920 feet) above sea-level. Beyond the valley-bottom town of Bollington, with its canal, and mills and houses all built from Kerridge stone, are Nab Head and the long scar of Moorside Quarry; and to the L the wide vista of the Cheshire Plain. It's fascinating to identify landmarks from up here with the aid of map and compass. Look for the white disc of Jodrell Bank radio telescope and the distant crag of Beeston Castle.

**SJ 939770** From White Nancy, follow the drystone wall along the ridge, towards a group of wind-swept beeches. Kerridge Hill is a knife-edged ridge that extends almost due north-south for about a mile-and-a-half (2.5 kms), from North End to Kerridge End in the south. The name Kerridge first appears in records in 1467 as *Caryge*, from the Old English words, *caeg* meaning stone and *hrycg* meaning ridge or back. Similarly, *cerrig* in Celtic Welsh means simply, stone. An important down-throw fault - a crack in the earth's surface - runs along the western flank of the ridge from Bollington towards the North Staffordshire coalfield. Along this fault the gritstones of the Peaks have pushed underneath the Carboniferous sandstones of Kerridge and buckled them upwards.

Beyond the trees, go through a gap in the stone wall and on along the ridge. Centuries of quarrying have eaten at the western edge, and the ground falls away sharply on either side. To the R is disused Gag Quarry; while to the L beech and larch trees huddle on the leeward side of the ridge, out of the wind. Beware of the quarry lip as the path winds along the edge; now invaded by sycamore saplings, the old workings below are over 25 metres (80 feet) deep.

**SJ 940768** Brambles and gnarled hawthorns protect the path from the wind. But soon the path edge is torn by subsidence as the topsoil slips away towards Sycamore Quarry. Below, the growl of huge mechanical diggers is punctuated by the high, ringing notes of hammer and chisel as skilled craftsmen split the pale sandstone; the finished roofing slabs are piled in steel boxes. Cranes and tripods angle out over the exposed rock faces. Run by a family firm, Sycamore Quarry still produces crazy paving, drystone walling, and dressing-stone for suburban gardens.

But the scene was not always so ordered. On the 14th of September 1777, the quarries were shaken by a violent earthquake centred around Macclesfield. *"Fair and fine, wind east, but very mild and hot"*, wrote a local farmer. He continued, *"At a few minutes before eleven I was attending divine service in church when occured a most sudden and violent trembling of the floor, which encreasing shooke the whole fabrick in a terrable manner, so that the church was expected to fall and burie us all."* Luckily for Kerridge, it was a Sunday. Had it happened on a weekday, the tremor would have killed most of the quarrymen.

**SJ 941765** Three hundred metres on, the path breasts a slight rise, then drops down into the Saddle of Kerridge. To the R of this hollow in the ridge a high, wire fence carries notices which warn: 'Danger. Fenced Quarry Face'. Disused Endon Quarries, far below, are now used as a shooting range.

**SJ 942763** Continue along the ridge for 200 metres, keeping the drystone wall to the L. Then go through a broad gap and over a stile. From here the hillside rises to the summit of the ridge, 320 metres (over 1,000 feet) above sea level. At the top the wind combs the wiry grass, and low hawthorns crouch, black against the eastern side of the hill. Now only 3 metres (10 feet) wide, the ridge narrows, carrying the path along its spine.

The views from the ridge to east and west are in complete contrast. The two landscapes - each determined by its underlying geology - are different. The Peaks are a maze of drystone walls; Cheshire fields are rimmed with hedges. To the east the panorama is mainly agricultural; industry scars the western view. Sheep nibble the Peaks' undulating

~~~~~~~~~~~~~~~~~~~~~~~~~~~~~~~~~~~~~~~~~~~~~~~~~~~

hills; while cattle browse on Cheshire's green plains. For want of a better metaphor, they are as alike as chalk and cheese.

**SJ 942759** A hundred metres along the ridge, go over a stile. Beyond is a white-painted OS triangulation point - a base from which to take the bearings used in map making. It also marks the highest point on the ridge. Far to the south, the view embraces the outlines of the Wrekin and Wenlock Edge, away in Shropshire. Hanging in the air like fragments of torn black cloth, crows tumble over the edge.

Beyond the 'trig' point, climb over an unusual stile with metal rungs set in wooden posts. To the R, is smaller Marksend Quarry. Jackdaws cackle above the edge. While below, large-wheeled diggers and a yellow Hy-Mac with a jack-hammer on the end of its hydraulic arm move about among the cutting sheds. The stone is pale and very hard; yet it splits easily along the bedding planes, and so has long been popular as a roofing material. Interestingly, Carboniferous fossils are sometimes found in the rock: shells, and sea-bed worm tracks and ripple marks. Look closely at the drystone wall beside the path: beneath the lichen the stone is pale yellow; and the bedding planes are well defined.

**SJ 944756** The path drops away along the slope of the ridge. The grass-softened pits of older stone workings dot the pasture. Three hundred metres from the stile, the path kinks to the R, and descends into a shallow, long-disused quarry. It's worth exploring. Notice how close to the surface the rock is, and how the nutrient-poor soil is as shallow as a tarpaulin draped across the ridge. The huge blocks of stone on the quarry floor also show clearly the strata of the bedding planes. On a windy day (and most days on Kerridge Ridge are windy) the grass is stroked out in curves and loops, revealing the air currents and eddies twisting over the quarry lip.

The path is clear, and dips obliquely downhill between coconut-scented, yellow-flowered gorse bushes. Leave the quarry over a stile at a gap in the drystone wall.

**SJ 944755** From here an incline descends the hill, falling gently across the contours of the slope. Broad and banked up by retaining drystone walls, it once carried the quarried stone away, downhill, probably in trucks mounted on a narrow-gauge railway. The wind soughs over the edge above, and black-faced sheep peer from the hawthorn thickets along the eastern flank of the hill. At the bottom of the slope, the track levels out beneath a row of tall ashes and sycamores. A path continues to the road.

**SJ 945754** But we double back to the L, along a bridleway that skirts the base of Kerridge Hill. From here, our route heads north, and seldom deviates from the contours of the slope. Beyond the fence to the R, sheep pastures dip away to Harrop Brook, a tributary stream of the River Dean.

**SJ 945755** Soon the path crosses a stile by a small gate, and runs on alongside a scrubby copse of holly and elder. Cut into the slope, the track is well defined and old. The view opens out, and below to the R is the tall, square chimney of derelict Cow Lane Mill. Once a silk mill, and then a bleach works, the ruins of the water-powered mill are hidden in the trees beside the River Dean. The village of Rainow, whose name in Anglo-Saxon meant 'Raven Hill', once had 24 mills, all long since gone.

**SJ 944760** Our path crosses another coming uphill from the mill - part of the Gritstone Trail. Go straight over, along the slope. Past the intersection, 75 metres on, and over a slight rise in the ground, is a sturdy, half-size wooden gate in a stone wall. Once through, follow the wall obliquely downhill to the R until, 150 metres later, it meets a well-defined path by a gate in the shadow of a holly tree. Go L towards the reservoir and Hough-hole Farm.

**SJ 943764** Across two more fields, the path rises slightly above a plantation of mixed conifers that shelters Kerridgeside House. High on Kerridge Hill's eastern slopes coal was once dug from opencast 'drift' mines and stone-lined shafts. It was dangerous and gruelling work, despite the use of donkeys to winch the coal to the surface. Packhorses with panniers carried the coal away to fuel the first steam-powered mills. Traces of fossil fish have been found in the old workings.

Past the plantation a small gate leads out onto open sheep-slopes. Part of the path across the field here is paved with Kerridge slabs - a common feature of local paths and a reminder of the days when most people walked to work.

**SJ 943767** Beneath a band of mature deciduous woodland, the path goes through a narrow gateway between two stone uprights. From here it heads out across the fields, where mushrooms grow, keeping 50 metres or so above the woodland edge along Ingersley Clough. Soon, tall ashes from an old hedgerow line the route; and the instantly recognisable shape of White Nancy tops the ridge up to the L.

**SJ 941771** At the far side of the field, go over a stile and then immediately R through a narrow gate marked with a yellow arrow. Turn L, past a fenced-off pond with ornamental wildfowl, and skirt North End Farm. Before the First World War the farm was worked by the eleven-strong Barlow family, but seven sons and a daughter emigrated to Canada. Two of the boys were killed in the war. One son and a daughter returned to Bollington; but the others stayed in Canada where they prospered.

Past the farm, go through a gate and on uphill to the L, along Independence Way. The farm drive continues around the end of the ridge, with White Nancy high on the hillside above. Stretched out below is the mill town of Bollington. Go over two cattle grids 250 metres apart, and then curve downhill to the L on Betty's Brew, and so back to the car park and the Redway Tavern.

It's a curious corner of Cheshire, more Peaks than plains. Yet for generations of Kerridge people, their lives shaped by the demands of cotton and stone, it has been home. Perhaps even for those who emigrated and never returned.

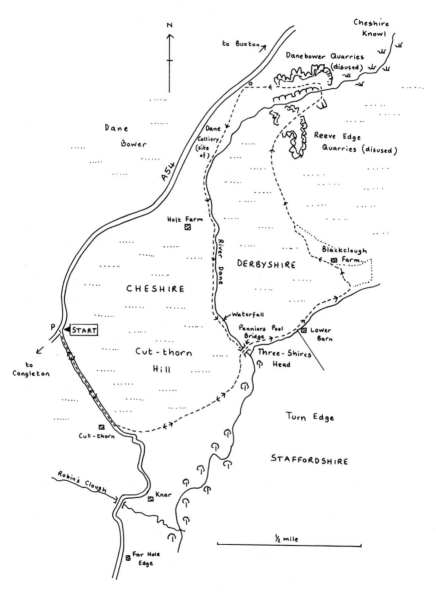

N

to Buxton

Cheshire
Knowl

Danebower Quarries
(disused)

Dane
Bower

Dane
Colliery
(site
of)

A54

Reeve Edge
Quarries (disused)

Holt Farm

River Dane

DERBYSHIRE

Blackclough
Farm

CHESHIRE

P
START

Waterfall

Panniers Pool
Bridge

Lower
Barn

to
Congleton

Cut-thorn
Hill

Three-Shires
Head

Turn Edge

Cut-thorn

STAFFORDSHIRE

Robin's Clough

Knar

½ mile

Far Hole
Edge

**Three Shires Head**

# 15 Three Shires Head ~ *where*
## *three counties meet ~*

Open moorland, River Dane valley, ancient packhorse bridge, hill farms and quarries.

---

**Start:** *Close to Cheshire's eastern border, 11 miles (18 kilometres) from Congleton, on the A54 Buxton road. Map reference* **SJ 999686.**

**Distance:** *4.5 miles (7 kilometres).*

**Duration:** *3 hours.*

**Maps:** *OS 1:50,000 Landranger Sheet 119; OS 1:25,000 Outdoor Leisure Sheet 24, The Peak District, White Peak Area; OS 1:25,000 SK 06.*

**Terrain:** *Rolling moorland; metalled lane, sandy track, boggy sheep slopes, riverside path. Wet and muddy in places.*

**Food and Drink:** *The Cat and Fiddle Inn (The second highest pub in England) on the A537 Macclesfield road. Map reference* **SK 001719.** *Robinsons. Meals and snacks. Children welcome in family room. Tel: Buxton 23364.*

---

Cheshire, Derbyshire and Staffordshire: three counties meet on an ancient packhorse bridge that spans a deep gorge in the Peak District, on Cheshire's eastern edge.

From Dane Head, its source on Axe Edge Moor, the crystal River Dane runs for 22 miles (35 kms) to join the River Weaver at Northwich, out on the Cheshire Plain. But long before it reaches the industrial bustle of the lowlands, the Dane tumbles over a lip of rock high on the moors, at the confluence of two upland streams. Isolated and idyllic, Three Shires Head is a hidden place that has long been a focus for events stretching far back into the past. Tough packhorse drivers called *jaggers*, itinerant peddlars, thieves, coin counterfeiters, deer poachers, criminals and prize-fighters have all met here. It's a scene steeped in history. Add to that its inherent wild beauty, and the surrounding moorland seamed with peat-black cloughs becomes a part of Cheshire that every walker ought to know.

**SJ 999686**  Our walk begins on the A54 Congleton to Buxton road as it climbs over bleak moorland past Allgreave and Wildboarclough. A mile-and-a-half (2 kms) from the Cheshire border, a minor road turns off below Cut-thorn Hill. Park in the small lay-by here, which has room for 4-5 cars.

Brown-streaked meadow pipits perch briefly on the drystone wall alongside the road; while slow-growing rosettes of grey lichen on the gritstone reflect the purity of the air. Looking back beyond the main road, the truncated cone of Shuttlingsloe, like some long-dead volcano or miniature Matterhorn, looms above the moor.

Follow the narrow road as it runs alongside 1,500 feet (460 metres) high Cut-thorn Hill. The unusual name comes from the old practice of cutting off all the branches of a living tree, to act as a boundary marker. Later there were three stone 'shire stones' on Cut-thorn Hill; but they have since disappeared. Black-faced sheep stare down from the open hillside to the L, at home among the peat  hummocks, sedge and bilberries. To the R, a skilled drystone-waller has left his signature in the form of a line of flat stones that jut stylishly from beneath the capstones of the head-high wall.

As the road dips downhill the view opens out ahead. On the closer slopes the geometric jigsaw lines of drystone walls are a long-term affirmation of generations-old farming techniques. They represent thousands of man-hours of dedicated labour. Beyond, the jagged teeth of the Roaches, Hen Cloud and the Bear Rocks are blue on the far horizon.

**SK 002681**  Half-a-mile (1 km) from the main road, branch off to the L up a rough track opposite Cut-thorn House. A sign announces it is 'Unsuitable For Traffic'. Swallows twist over the rocky slopes above in summer, while several distinct sheep notes rise from the pastures that slope down towards the Dane. A distant rushing of water fills the valley; and a winding line of dark sycamores and alders marks the route of the river.

**SK 009685** Within another half-a-mile (1 km) the sandy, gritstone track descends to the River Dane, and we can look down upon the shallow, babbling waters. At the bottom of the slope four paths meet at an ancient packhorse bridge, framed by the bright splashes of orange rowan berries. The silence is almost tangible; the only sounds are natural: sheep, water, birds and insects.

*An ancient packhorse bridge spans Panniers Pool at Three Shires Head, where three counties meet.*

157

# Three Shires Head Packhorse Bridge

*A sign stating that this is a 'Public Bridleway' points across the bridge. It's a distant echo of the days when packhorse strings, perhaps with panniers - or side baskets - full of salt from the Cheshire 'wiches', would meet here on their journey over the hills to Buxton. Today, the pool below the bridge is still called Panniers pool.*

*In the 14th century the flat piece of ground beside Three Shires Bridge was the site of a court held to hear evidence against people accused of trespass in the royal Forest of Macclesfield. The Lord of the Forest, the Black Prince, ordered that, "tenants of the counties of Derby and Stafford who are indicted of trespass in the said forest shall come with the steward, and that those whom the lieutenant shall on examination find guilty of such trespasses shall give satisfaction as reason demands." Whether such satisfaction was a fine, or death, is uncertain.*

*Much later, in the 1860s and '70s, the same piece of flat ground was the venue for illegal prize fights. Victorian society had become disgusted by the brutality and unfair practices of these bare-knuckle pugilists, and Marquis of Queensbury rules were introduced to the 'sport'. Nonetheless, its popularity in country areas took some time to die out, especially when purses as high as £200 were on offer. Three Shires Head was chosen as the site for these popular but savage contests because, at the first sign of either local constables or magistrates, both the contestants and the large crowd of excited punters around the roped-off ring could skip across the boundaries into either of two other counties.*

**SK 010685** Over the bridge, go straight ahead, through an iron gate. You have now left Cheshire. A rough, boulder-strewn path climbs on uphill. Tall scots pines and hornbeams clothe the opposite slope, above the tributary stream which bickers in its deep cutting to the R. The rocks, beneath fern-clad banks, are stained a curious rusty brown by iron in the water.

**SK 012686** Where the track levels, 300 metres on, a stone bridge crosses the stream on a bend. It leads off past Lower Barn, towards Knotbury End Farm and Wolf Edge.

But we go L, on along the broader track that hugs the stream. Already the area has an upland feel. Ahead, on the bunched hills above the stream, the dark windows of Black Clough and Orchard Farm watch our slow approach. A track cuts sharply up to the L, but we walk on through a gate. Beside it the stream gurgles over steps in the bedrock.

**SK 015688** Now surfaced with rough limestone chippings, the narrow track climbs once more, to emerge on a metalled farm lane. Turn L, up a steep tarmaced drive to Blackclough Farm; it's also a public footpath, marked on the map. At the top go through a gate, through the farmyard, and past the farm.

Farms like these have to rely on their own resources in hard winters. Back in 1947 the Dane Valley was hopelessly snow-bound for 14 weeks, and relief vans filled with food from Macclesfield could get no closer than the Ryles Arms, an inn two miles (3 kms) north of Cleulow Cross. Undaunted, the farmers brought out their sleighs to collect supplies, handing over their churns of milk in return.

**SK 013690** At the end of the farmyard, a second gate leads out into boggy fields. Go straight ahead, keeping the drystone wall on your L for the next 150 metres. At the next gateway, head diagonally out to your R, across the rough, thistle-strewn sheep pasture. (The path is marked clearly on the Outdoor Leisure map). A drystone wall up to the R disappears over the brow of the slope; but 250 metres later there is a gateway, clear between tall stone posts.

Look back. Given the right conditions, the Welsh mountains are clearly visible. In 1842 when the original Ordnance Survey was being made, a heliographic reflector on top of Lincoln Cathedral, 70 miles (112 kms) to the east, was used by the surveyors as a triangulation point. Forty years later, when the traveller Edward Bradbury crossed *"this savage wilderness"* in 1883, he claimed it was possible to see seven counties. He was obviously impressed. *"All around"*, he wrote, *"is the spell of silence, the sense of space, the scent of thyme and heather."*

**SK 012692** Beyond the gap, go L, and follow the sturdy wall as it curves away downhill. The lamenting calls of curlews punctuate the moorland slopes above. Ahead are the Dane valley and, following the contours of the hills beyond, the A54 grinding up towards Buxton. Below the road is a tall square chimney that was once part of the now disused Dane Bower quarries. When, 350 metres later, the wall ends at a sharp corner, look for a square hole covered with a drystone slab lintel: it's a 'sheep creep', designed to allow the farmer to block or open access for his sheep to different parts of the hills.

**SK 011698** Ahead, 150 metres from the corner of the wall, the path forks. Go L, over a small rise and downhill into the Reeve Edge quarries. Curved, inturned drystone walls, like the revetments of some Iron Age hillfort, form an entrance to these disused works, where piles of shattered grey stone are speckled with smokey lichen. From here came the stone to build the once flourishing silk mill downstream at Gradbach, as well as the many cottages of the workers. The mill is now a Youth Hostel. There used also to be a coal pit upstream at Dane Bower, close to the source of the Dane, one of a number in the area that was worked within living memory.

**SK 014700** The rough path runs on obliquely down the slope, past the remains of the quarrymen's tiny houses and work sheds, to meet the 6 feet (2 metres) wide infant Dane, beneath towering spoil heaps. Upstream, the narrow river vanishes in a waste of bog and sedge. Crude stepping stones across the narrow stream and a scramble up a rocky bank, lead to the Dane Bower Quarries, back in Cheshire.

At the top of the bank is a circular blasting shelter, now without its roof. Beyond, and to the L, a ramp of compacted rubble climbs up onto the top of the spoil heaps. From now on, we follow the Dane downstream. But first, it's worth exploring the quarries; among other delights, a shallow waterfall here feeds a boggy area that becomes a small lake in winter.

**SK 010700**   A broad track winds between the spoil heaps. Two hundred metres before the A54, a clear path branches off to the L, parallel to the river, and snakes downhill to a stile beneath the dark finger of the chimney.

**SK 009696**   Soon the path widens once more into a grassy track above the Dane. Closer to the river, sit awhile and listen to the different voices of the stream. Grey wagtails, with their yellow breasts, nest sometimes beneath the ferny overhangs of the bank; and tiny brown trout flicker in the whisky-coloured water of the deeper pools.

Past Holt Farm, framed by the fretted silhouettes of tall sycamores, the path climbs over a stile into the gentle pastures of these lower slopes, and then runs alongside the river for a while. Over another stile the slope steepens imperceptibly, and the Dane cuts itself a deeper valley.

**SK 008691**   A narrow bridge traverses a side stream; empty in summer, the rock-filled cleft is white with water after winter rains. Other watercourses tumble down the bracken-clad slopes to the R of the path above the river, some reinforced in places by the judicious use of concrete. A little further on and we are back at Three Shires Head, where the centuries-old packhorse bridge straddles the Dane above Panniers Pool.

We've come full circle. Pause once more to take in the tranquility of the scene, and to recall the varied history of this moorland meeting place. And then retrace the outward route, back up the rutted path around Cut-thorn Hill. In the dust, the double, slotted prints of countless sheep are mingled with the crescent-shaped shoe-marks of horses - the modern ancestors of the thousands of animals that once helped to make Three Shires Head such an important crossroads on the moors at Cheshire's eastern edge.

# Further Reading

**Bullock, J.D.** Pre-Conquest Cheshire 383-1066, Chester, 1972.

**Coward, T.A.** Cheshire, Cambridge, 1910.

**Crossley, Fred. H.** Cheshire, London, 1949.

**Crump, W.B.** Saltways from the Cheshire Wiches, Trans. Lancs. & Ches. Ant. Soc. LIV, 1939.

**Dodgson, J.McN.** The Place Names of Cheshire, Vols I-IV, Cambridge, 1970.

**Driver, J.L.** Cheshire in the Later Middle Ages, Chester, 1971.

**Harris, B.E.** (ed.) The Victoria County History of Cheshire, Vol II, Oxford, 1979.

**Hughes, Herbert.** Cheshire and its Welsh Border, London, 1966.

**Husain, B.M.C.** Cheshire Under the Norman Earls, Chester, 1973.

**Kelly's Directory of Cheshire,** Annually.

**Ormerod, G.** The History of the County Palatine and City of Chester, 3 vols, 2nd edition, ed by T. Helsby, 1882.

**Richards, Raymond.** Old Cheshire Churches, London, 1947.

**Stephens, W.B.** (ed.) History of Congleton, Manchester, 1970.

**Sylvester, D. & Nutty, G.** The Historical Atlas of Cheshire. Cheshire Community Council, 1958.

**Thompson, F.H.** Roman Cheshire, Chester, 1965.

**Varley, W.J.** Cheshire before the Romans, Chester, 1964.

**Varley, W.J.** Recent Investigations into the Origins of Cheshire Hill Forts, Trans. Lancs. & Ches. Ant. Soc. LI, 1936.

**Watkins, W.T.** Roman Cheshire, Liverpool, 1886.

# Index

~~~~~~~~~~~~~~~~~~~~~~~~~~~~~~~~~~~~~~~~~~~~~~~~~~~~

~~~~~~~~~~~~~~~~~~~~~~~~~~~~~~~~~~~~~~~~~~~~~~~~~

# About the Author

The Author Tony Bowerman is a professional freelance advertising copywriter who lives in Chester. A postgraduate of Durham University, he has worked both at Warrington Museum and as a copywriter in industry.

Features and articles of his have appeared in, among others, Cheshire Life, Cheshire Vista, Cheshire Today, The Cheshire Times, The Countryman, The Searcher and the children's comic Oink! Until its untimely demise, he wrote a weekly nature column in The North-West Times.

As a copywriter, Tony Bowerman writes anything from brochures to business manuals, but specialises in guides, walks, trails and information packs for both adults and children. He can be contacted via the Publishers or directly on Chester (0244) 378927.